The Magic of Mess Painting

The Creativity Mobilization Technique

by
Virginia Barclay Goldstein

Trans-Hyperborean Institute of Science
P.O. Box 2344, Sausalito, California 94966 USA
Phone: (415) 331-0230 Fax: (415) 331-0231
Book website: http://t-hyp.com/messpainting, Publisher website: http://t-hyp.com
email to Virginia at: virginia@t-hyp.com

If you are unable to find this book in your local bookstore, you may order it from the publisher. Quantity discounts for organizations are available. Call: 1-(800) 485-8095.

First Printing August 1999

10 9 8 7 6 5 4 3 2 1

Library of Congress Cataloging-in-Publication Data

Goldstein, Virginia
The Magic of Mess PaintinG
p. 224
Includes bibliography and index

ISBN: 0-9657825-4-9

1. Creation (Literary, artistic, etc.)
2. Self-Actualization (Psychology)
3. Art Therapy

LC# 99-61323

DISCLAIMER

The purpose of this book is to educate and entertain. The author and Trans-Hyperborean Institute of Science shall have neither liability nor responsibility to any person or entity with respect to any loss or damage caused, or alleged to be caused, directly or indirectly, by the information contained in this book.

The information written is based on the personal experiences, observations and research of the author, who is not a medical doctor. The practices and techniques described are not to be used as an alternative to professional medical treatment. The book does not attempt to give any medical diagnosis, treatment, or suggestion in relation to any human disease, pain, injury, deformity, or physical condition. If you have a mental illness or disorder, a medical doctor or psychologist should be consulted before you start painting.

Anyone who undertakes these painting exercises does so entirely at his or her own risk. Pregnant women, people with high blood pressure, heart disease, or a generally weak condition should consult a physician before practicing any of the exercises.

If you do not wish to be bound by the above, you may return this book to the publisher for a full refund.

Virginia Barclay Goldstein

Virginia Barclay Goldstein is a psychotherapist who facilitates the Creativity Mobilization Technique (CMT), also known as Mess Painting, with individuals and groups.

She received a combined BFA from the Chicago Art Institute and the University of Chicago. She later earned her Master's degree in rehabilitation counseling from San Francisco State University, and was licensed as a Marriage and Family Counselor in 1975. She has been a professional member of the American Art Therapy Association since its inception.

In the early days of the Esalen Institute, Virginia was instructed by Fritz Perls, the father of Gestalt psychology, in an art therapy technique called Painting with Partners. She went on to employ this dynamic method with groups of healthy adults, and also with mentally disturbed patients in a day treatment setting. She presented a paper on this clinical work and its positive results at an international conference on art and psychopathology in Paris in 1967.

Virginia studied CMT with its creator Dr. Wolfgang Luthe (1922-1985), a German-born research physician famous for his contribution to Autogenic Training and Therapy, which included six volumes of research co-authored with Johannes Schultz and published by Grune and Stratton, who also published Luthe's book on CMT. Following Dr. Luthe's death in 1985, Virginia has become the foremost authority on the Creativity Mobilization Technique. She is also an honorary member of the British Autogenic Society.

She recently retired from the American Art Therapy Association and went on inactive status as an MFC, preferring to limit her private practice to guiding functioning people in the use of CMT to accelerate their process of self-actualization. Her experience with CMT is documented in a film, *The Creativity Mobilization Technique*.

Acknowledgments

I wish to thank my deceased husband Norman Goldstein for his consistent powerful support of my work, without which I would not have started this book. The years of working with my editor, Kathy Goss, have been a joy. Her enthusiasm about the ultimate success of the project carried us through many unexpected interruptions. I wish to thank Kathryn Ann Dudley for all her help during those painful times and for her unpaid and persistent promotion of CMT with everyone she knows. I have been very fortunate to work with Jennifer Dumm of the Trans-Hyperborean Institute of Science on layout, graphics, cover design, and all of the business arrangements involved in publishing.

My gratitude to Elizabeth Atwood Taylor, Don and Eugenia Gerrard, Michael Greene, Stephanie Cress, Virginia Jouis, Joan Peirce, Sally Salans, Lucie Duranceau, Steven R. Blumberger, and J.L.G. de Rivera for their assistance in the critical early stages of writing this book.

My blessings to John Curry and Janice Crow for persuading people in the Sonoma, California area to undertake Mess Painting, and to my English colleagues, especially Vera Diamond and Jane Bird, for their impatient insistence that I finish this book so that CMT can flourish in Great Britain.

Many heartfelt thanks to the friends, relatives, and CMT participants — some identified by their real names, some by pseudonyms, some unnamed — whose stories, paintings, and loving assistance have breathed life into this book.

CONTENTS

Introduction

by Gay Luce, Ph.D.

This book is one of those great, long-awaited tools that will be treasured in decades to come. It offers the reader a chance to do a process that is utterly transforming, and is always appropriate for the individual. Unlike many self-help books, this one goes deep into the regions of the unconscious that most of us cannot easily access, and into blocks we believed we could not change on our own.

One of the most unexpectedly inspiring and rewarding experiences of my life has been the process described in this book, the Creativity Mobilization Technique, or CMT — also known as Mess Painting. It uses art materials, but not deliberately to create art. Rather the idea is to generate internal processes leading to insight, self-healing, and creativity.

It was in 1975 that Virginia Goldstein and I first made the acquaintance of Dr. Wolfgang Luthe, the developer of Autogenic Training, and later, of the Creativity Mobilization Technique. At Dr. Luthe's invitation, Virginia and I followed the instructions in his as-yet unpublished manuscript, painting almost daily for seven weeks. It was an exhilarating, emotional, and revealing experience. I noticed that I might get up in the morning in a sullen mood, or with a feeling of stuckness. As I began painting I could often feel the energy move out of my throat and through my arms — as anger, then excitement, then exaltation, sometimes even ecstasy. I could see this change of mood in the paintings. Some of the results were astounding. Without intent — I was, after all, just Mess Painting — landscapes, skyscapes, nudes, flowers, and haunting abstract images emerged, seemingly on their own. I looked forward to these painting sessions. Strangely, my friends asked me to let them have paintings that they particularly liked.

Later I did Mess Painting on my own, following the structure that Luthe had given us, and I repeated the sessions yet again some years later in a friend's garage, while attending one of Virginia's CMT groups.

After listening to many people who have come through the CMT process, I believe that it is one of the most versatile healing modalities we have. It surely takes the restrictive wraps off the inner being, freeing energy, creativity, artistic pleasure, and confidence.

For many of us, CMT offers the first time since childhood that we can really play without thinking about cleanliness, or time, or results. In our results-oriented culture the possibility of taking some time for utter spontaneity is already a step toward inner freedom. The enlivening impact of bright colors on the brain, the unbinding of suppressed or numbed feelings, along with the movements of the body, provide an infusion of vitality, clarity, and infinite potentiality. Sometimes I look back with awe on the transcendent states that opened up during CMT, as the brush sent a skylike wash of blue, a streak of spring pink, spraying across the newsprint, and a scent of jasmine and an electric shimmer announced the unity of my vaporous body with everything that is.

CMT is a method that can be done at home. Unlike most therapies, no one outside of your own nervous system is prompting a response, interpreting, or imposing a system. You become your own healer, your own observer, trusting the unfoldment of some inherent wisdom and beauty which is simply waiting to be discovered.

We all owe thanks to Virginia for the continuous dedication, guidance, and research out of which this book emerges. It has kept alive a precious contribution to human happiness and greater consciousness. Without Luthe it wouldn't have formed; without Virginia it could have died. At long last here is a readable book to guide you into CMT (Luthe's book is academic in the extreme), with a videotape available to show Mess Painters in action.

I personally believe that this book will have a very long life, and will become one of those classic tools for self-discovery that people keep in their homes, the way they have a fundamental cookbook and a first aid manual. Not that CMT is at that basic a level; but I think that expanding consciousness will become more of a staple requirement of life as we move beyond the millennium.

- Gay Luce, Ph.D., Psychologist,
Director of the Nine Gates Mystery School

Chapter One

Invitation to an Adventure

"We make progress by a constant spiraling back and forth between the inner world and the outer one, the personal and the political, the self and the circumstance. Nature doesn't move in a straight line and, as a part of nature, neither do we."
- Gloria Steinem

Are you itching for something new in your life? Are you feeling stuck, depressed, dissatisfied with your work or your relationships? Are you having difficulty getting in touch with your feelings, or upset about some negative family or job situation?

Let me share with you an amazing, almost magical technique for stimulating self-healing and self-renewal and awakening creativity. It is known as Mess Painting, or the Creativity Mobilization Technique. As the above quotation suggests, it is through a "spiraling back and forth between the inner world and the outer one" that we move forward. Mess Painting is a powerful hands-on tool for taking us on this spiraling course of personal evolution. This book will show you how, using paint, brush, and paper, you can increase your self-knowledge and self-confidence, relieve emotional distress, and release the creativity within you.

Mess Painting is concerned with freedom — freedom to express emotion, to satisfy your needs, to say "Yes, yes" to life. It requires a private space, preferably one where yelling or singing would be equally possible; eight colors of tempera paint; eight children's thick round brushes; and a stack of old newspapers.

The brush is held in such a way that brush, hand, and arm work together as an extension of the whole body. Standing to paint permits the entire body to participate. Depending on your emotional state, you may make dance-like gestures with long, rhythmical, gentle brush strokes, or you may attack the painting — hitting it with the brush so hard that dramatic splashes of paint land on the plastic-covered walls and on yourself, as well as on the paper.

Mess Painting sounds deceptively simple at first, but it is the point of departure in a carefully researched method of developing creativity functions. It is a way of learning to shift gears out of your usual thinking-analyzing state of mind and beginning to learn how to listen to yourself, pay attention, and be involved without any attempt to predict or control outcomes.

Painting in this way connects us to the visual, spatial, intuitive, non-verbal part of ourselves that is generally neglected in this society, and that seems to be where our "inner healer" resides.

In Mess Painting there is no planning or execution of any forms, no building on emerging patterns, and no image making. What is important is to get rid of product making and be totally engaged with painting as process. You are to "let go" and paint without any desire or concern about the outcome.

As you follow the carefully designed instructions this becomes easy to do, and moreover it is a lot of fun. The sense of freedom, the spontaneity that Mess Painting engenders flows into ordinary life, bringing unexpected positive changes.

"Creativity may be broadly defined as the ability and facility to actually produce, make or express something that, at least in part, originated from oneself."

- Wolfgang Luthe

Before going into the myriad practical details that form a safe structure within which this "letting go" with paint takes place, I want to tell you a bit about myself. This is important, for without knowing an author's views and values, without getting a feel for the author as a person, how are you to evaluate adequately the recommended technique, particularly one that is to be done on your own? Professional qualifications by themselves seem insufficient to me.

And so, I propose to show you how my own spiraling course led me to embrace the Creativity Mobilization Technique, or CMT, as the focus of my professional life.

My Spiraling Journey

I have always believed that participation in the arts is normal, natural, and beneficial for everyone. I was fortunate to grow up in a family where the arts were appreciated and practiced. My parents, despite their modest income, encouraged me to pursue a fine arts degree, perhaps not the most practical choice during the years of the Great Depression.

All the women in my family, more so than the men, traveled abroad, and those of my generation had the *chutzpa* to defy the behavioral rules of the time and travel alone rather than with a friend or chaperone, or on a guided tour. During the summer between my junior and senior years of college I freely wandered by myself through Northern Europe, as far east as Hungary, then down the Dalmatian Coast to Albania, before experiencing the aesthetic riches of Italy and France. Upon completing my studies at the Chicago Art Institute and the University of Chicago I sought and found an adventurous life in the art world of California.

In 1940 at the San Francisco World's Fair, while demonstrating silkscreen printing in the Art in Action Pavilion, I met the Greek painter Jean Varda. I was fascinated not only by Varda's beautiful, sensual work, but also by the man himself. At forty-eight he was many years my senior — handsome, a great dancer, and a captivating natural storyteller. He was extremely well educated, albeit self-taught, and his wisdom had a deeply spiritual base.

Wherever he lived he created a charming environment without succumbing to modern consumerism. Despite his lack of money he almost always had complete control of his time and therefore the freedom to paint as many hours as he wished, night and day.

Understanding that I could learn a lot from this man, I went to live with Varda on the Big Sur coast south of Carmel, in the barracks-like structure that had housed the convicts who had built the recently completed Big Sur Coast highway. Five weeks later, on my twenty-fourth birthday, we held a huge costume ball, and at midnight exchanged our marriage vows.

Following the Japanese attack on Pearl Harbor we were not allowed to live on the coast, and moved to nearby Monterey. There we eventually bought a magnificent old redwood barn, in whose former hayloft we held our costumed dancing parties. I set up a pottery studio downstairs in the former stable, and in the old carriage room Varda created his unusual collages. Drawn by Varda's brilliant conversation, visitors came almost daily. Henry Miller — whose *"unconventional lifestyle and outrageous writing inspired the Bohemians and writers who in turn expanded their freedom and altered social behavior in America forever"*[1] — was our house guest for several weeks while he looked for a place of his own in Big Sur. On his arrival he was visibly disappointed to discover that Varda's wife was not a black-haired, big-eyed, full-hipped Greek woman but rather a young, blonde, long-legged American. Nevertheless, we became friends.

Henry appreciated my giving him the dining room for his writing and painting space. I enjoyed watching him paint his delightful watercolors and hearing him discourse on art and the artists he knew. Today I ask all my CMT clients to read excerpts from his essays on art. Miller painted for the sheer pleasure of taking up the brush *"to see what happens."* Turning off what he called the thinking machine, he would move into a state of being in which, as he put it, *"to paint is to love again, live again, see again."*

When Varda and I divorced, I moved to San Francisco with my infant daughter. After several years of depressing and tedious work as a draftsman in electrical engineering offices, I sought therapy to rebuild my relationship to my inner and outer worlds. Nothing seemed to help until I encountered Dr. Milton Erickson, an extraordinary psychiatrist who was using hypnosis and intensive short-term therapy long before they became common in psychological and psychiatric practice. He saw me two hours each day for almost two weeks. Those sessions radically changed my life, shook up my inner world and cleared away the "garbage" that had blocked access to my healthy core, my self-confidence and clarity of mind and emotion.

With the gift of my sudden and profound awakening through Erickson's therapy, I was wide open to new possibilities. I applied to a graduate program in rehabilitation counseling at San Francisco State University. I still have to smile when I recall the interview for admission to the program. One of the three professors asked, "What have you ever done for people?" Stymied for a moment, I recovered and blurted out, "The only thing I've ever done for people is give great parties." To my astonishment my spontaneous, honest reply seemed to please them. I now realize that those "great parties" were an early expression of my supporting people in their exploration of the unfettered, unstructured, free part of themselves and their connection to others. I now understand that this is what CMT can help people do, in a deeper way, for themselves.

After graduation I got a job at an innovative day treatment center for the mentally ill. There I had the freedom to introduce art therapy techniques instead of being restricted to using my counseling skills. About that time I also studied at the Esalen Institute with Fritz Perls, the

"Ask yourself this question now: Am I living by deadlines - or by lifelines? Living by lifelines is living by intention, rather than by accident."[2]

- Marcia Pear

father of Gestalt psychology. One afternoon Fritz asked me to direct the group in an exercise called "Painting with Partners" while he took a nap. Group members chose as partners those whom they felt they knew the least. The partners then took turns painting *in silence* on one large piece of news-print until both agreed, through gestures, that the painting was finished. After the whole group had finished painting each pair reported on their experi-ences. Their intense reactions and lively confrontations vividly demonstrated that painting freely with brilliant colors can be a powerful catalyst for evoking feelings. This provocative technique had the elements of self-confrontation, freedom, and fun that I would later encounter in Mess Painting.

Back at the day treatment center I set up an eight-week pilot study to investigate the effects of scheduling a Painting with Partners session immedi-ately preceding the twice-weekly group therapy hour, attended by fourteen adult patients. The therapists, a social worker and a psychologist, were de-lighted with the results. The painting sessions brought out "here-and-now" behavior that could be worked with in the following hour. In addition the patients were less indifferent to each other, and the increased interaction made their therapy sessions more productive.

I created an exhibit and wrote a paper on my successful pilot study, which I presented in Paris in 1967 at the Fifth Congress of the International Society of Art and Psychopathology. While this trip convinced me more than ever of the benefits of focusing on art materials in my work, I also took the practical step of working toward a Marriage, Family and Child Counseling (MFCC) license, which I received in 1975.

In 1967 I married Norman N. Goldstein, a connoisseur of classical music and poetry, as well as a professor of physiology. Both of us were very interested in alternative modes of healing — acupuncture, homeopathy, vari-ous types of bodywork, and the Monroe Institute audio tapes.

Early in 1975, with Norman's encouragement, I had begun my in-ternship for becoming a Marriage, Family, and Child Counselor. In Sep-tember he urged me to attend the National Conference of the American Association for Psychophysiology and Biofeedback in Monterey with my friend, psychologist Gay Luce[3]. At the conference I met Wolfgang Luthe, M.D., a highly respected German-born research physician and authority on psychophysiology, who was the co-developer of Autogenic Training. In his presentation at the conference Luthe enthusiastically described the positive outcomes that resulted from using Autogenic Training and Therapy for a variety of physical and psychological problems. He said that patients with psychosomatic symptoms often had to unload depressing and traumatic memories, especially previously totally repressed ones, before complete healing could take place. As part of their homework, he frequently assigned his patients a special painting process, which he called the Creativity Mobilization Technique, or CMT, to stimulate this catharsis.

Intrigued, Gay and I arranged to meet privately with Luthe during the conference to learn more about this painting technique. He generously offered to send us a copy of the manuscript of a textbook on CMT that he had recently completed, so that we need not wait for the book to come out to explore the method for ourselves. We gratefully accepted his offer.

My First Encounter with Mess Painting

Back at home, Luthe's manuscript soon arrived. Carefully following the instructions, Gay and I took turns painting alone in my studio. We had great fun during our solitary painting sessions; in fact, a painting from that period still hangs in my home.

On most occasions I ended my painting sessions feeling happy and energized, but at other times I ended feeling irritable, even nauseous. These negative reactions were upsetting and baffling. Unfortunately, it had not occurred to me to make an arrangement with Dr. Luthe to send him paintings (home video was not available to me then) and get his feedback. Had I done so my initial experience with CMT would have been quite different.

I realized at the end of the prescribed seven weeks of painting that I still did not know enough about CMT to use it with others. Since the method seemed to offer so much more than the art therapy techniques I had been using in my private practice, I decided to study with Luthe in Montreal, where he now made his home.

In Montreal I painted every day, getting to know Luthe as a compassionate and humorous man, as well as an exacting professor. Before I left, as part of his requirements for becoming a certified CMT facilitator, I took his exam. I continued with Mess Painting on my own, and Luthe provided some long-distance supervision with my first clients. Later I was placed on the International Advisory Board for the Teaching of the Creativity Mobilization Technique.

The year 1976 found me at a critical point, a crossroads, needing to define my goals. Now a newly licensed Marriage, Family, and Child Counselor, I wrote to Dr. Milton Erickson describing the Creativity Mobilization Technique and its ability to evoke memories of early traumatic episodes, often ones never before called forth. I asked his advice on making CMT my life's work instead of developing a counseling practice. Erickson's short, non-directive, subtly affirmative reply was handwritten: "*Real psychotherapy is helping people to get in touch with their learnings, intentional, indirect and experiential, many of which are not recognized or even known.*"

Those words made my choice easier, and I've never regretted my decision. Facilitating creativity and seeing people make all sorts of positive changes has given me my "right livelihood."

Only a few practitioners trained by Luthe or myself are available at this time to assist people in exploring CMT. Because of Luthe's difficult writing style and publisher's errors in labeling the color plates, his book did not prove to be an effective self-help tool; nor did it attract professionals to study with him. It has been out of print for many years.

To ensure that CMT will endure beyond my life span, I wrote the present book with its guidelines, philosophy, and precise instructions to provide adventurous, disciplined individuals with an opportunity for a very unusual and beneficial experience. For those who desire further support, I offer the opportunity to obtain guidance from me by correspondence (see Epilogue). I hope this book will attract freedom-loving health professionals, art therapists, and art instructors to use the CMT process for themselves. Additionally I hope some will be inspired to become certified CMT facilitators so that they can competently help suitable clients or students to receive maximum benefit from undertaking the Creativitiy Mobilization Technique. I will be conducting courses for this purpose.

Overview of the Creativity Mobilization Technique

Is CMT Art Therapy? I have been a registered art therapist with the American Art Therapy Association for many years, and I have great respect for my colleagues and their accomplishments. Because CMT uses art materials, many people wrongly assume it is art therapy. I believe calling CMT a form of art therapy does nothing to clarify either approach. Knowing how they differ is important, for there are situations where art therapy would be much more suitable than CMT, and vice versa.

For example, CMT is not suitable for weekend or week-long workshops, because it must be done on one's own and because it requires a much longer time commitment. I continue to use art therapy techniques, including Painting with Partners, in workshops with organizations — particularly, over the past eight years, with Refocus, a Marin County organization whose founder, Rae Ellen Godfrey, has been extremely successful in empowering men and women who are not living up to their potential to restructure their lives in positive ways.

The development of CMT began in the late 1940s, whereas art therapy reaches back to Jung and Freud and has been a separate discipline since World War II. Art therapy has been used successfully for the diagnosis and treatment of diverse populations that include, but are not limited to, families, autistic children, the mentally ill, the learning disabled, and the aged. Art therapy is also used in a variety of ways in medical settings, including with terminally ill cancer patients and in burn units.

The Creativity Mobilization Technique cannot be used as a diagnostic tool, and the population it serves is different from that served by art therapy.

When correctly applied with "well people who want to be weller," it is extremely effective.

You may ask what I mean by "well." I think "well" includes almost all of us — i.e., those who don't have a history of psychosis, who are able to follow instructions, who manage to earn a living, who have relationships and function as best they can in this unpredictable world. Prospective CMT participants, however, do need to have a tolerance for ambivalence and ambiguity and to feel intact psychologically, because the CMT experience may evoke psychological and physiological phenomena that need to be explored and integrated.

For further comparisons between the CMT and art therapy I will quote a young woman who suffered considerable abuse and deprivation in her childhood, yet with courage and determination had made a place for herself in the business world. This achievement was not enough to establish a sense of self-worth, and suspecting she was still influenced by her past, she attempted to overcome its effects with standard verbal psychotherapy. After two months of treatment she decided to quit her psychologist and seek out an art therapist a friend had recommended. Ten sessions of art therapy satisfied her needs at that time. A year later she opted to continue her personal evolution with CMT. Sarah clearly remembered and was very grateful for her encounters with art therapy and CMT, and was quite willing to talk about the differences between them:

"In my art therapy sessions when I had a hard time making a choice as to which medium I would use, my art therapist would make a suggestion and when I was working on a picture she would often say a few words of encouragement.

"In CMT I painted at home alone. Doing this was like flying blind and, at times, quite scary. No one was present to tell me I mixed the paint too thin or too thick. But I gradually found meeting the challenge of working on my own exciting.

"While Mess Painting, when I was dealing with negative subjects I would groan, weep, swear, yell, etc. In my art therapy sessions I cried at times or hummed, but vocal expression was minimal compared to what happened in Mess Painting.

"I loved the kinesthetic aspect of Mess Painting — the way my whole body

was involved. In art therapy I sat at a table and used mainly finger and hand motions but I certainly didn't swing my arms or stomp my feet.

"I found the thick, expensive white paper provided by the art therapist intimidating, whereas newspaper is a waste item. Besides, it had an additional advantage in that a headline or a picture could trigger a memory or a feeling.

"When I saw the word 'MONEY' dramatized in two-inch-high white capitals on a black background, it hit me like a slap in the face .... I went for it .... As I covered it with green paint, I was wild with the frustration I've always had about the stuff ... never enough ... seemingly no way to earn a decent amount. The green paint, always my least favorite of the CMT colors, was now loathsome. Maybe if I covered sheet after sheet I could get rid of it and money forever ... fat chance . . . but I tried until I was limp and suddenly the anger vanished. Thoughts about money vanished. I could care less. Green was just green and I laughed."

The first time Sarah admitted her true feelings about her abusive father was in an art therapy session. She was astonished to discover this rage simmering under a virtually lifelong struggle against depression.

Sarah's rage against her father came up again full force in more than one Mess Painting session, indicating that the time constraint of the art therapy hour had forced her to move to the cognitive level too quickly. She had needed more time just to be with her emotions. In Mess Painting she was able to stay with the anger and fear that the spontaneous use of colors had triggered, and with the buried memories connected to those feelings.

Art therapy was very helpful in uncovering Sarah's problems, but it was the kinesthetic quality of CMT that allowed the physical abuse she had suffered and held in her body to unwind and be neutralized.

In Mess Painting Sarah found a situation conducive to dwelling deeply and fully with her emotions, and also one which allowed the wild side of her nature to emerge. Since she painted in private, she could quite safely be silly, crazy, illogical, impetuous. She could howl as she had never done before. In Mess Painting Sarah found her own strong, untamed woman. She welcomed her presence, understanding that it would be a positive, creative force in her life.

The Painting Process

The first practical consideration in deciding whether or not to undertake CMT is whether or not you have, or could borrow or rent, a suitable place in which to paint. The work area needs to be a place where the setup can remain for two months or longer, without having to be put away each time. Ideally, the work space should have sufficient privacy for making sounds — singing, swearing, crying, whistling — without bothering anyone else. I cannot overstate the importance of having a safe, protected, private area in which to be playful or to act out powerful emotions while painting.

Typically a CMT program takes seven weeks, with four painting sessions a week. During each session approximately fifteen to twenty paintings are made, spending up to, but no more than, two minutes on each painting before it is placed to dry. Occasionally more than twenty paintings are created in order to allow the emotions that have surfaced to be fully expressed. The painting is done on full spread sheets of *The Wall Street Journal* because it is generally the largest and widest newspaper readily available in this country. This size or larger encourages and facilitates making the desired extended arm movements while painting.

The paint is water-based school tempera bought by the gallon in eight colors: black, white, brown, red, yellow, blue, green, and violet. There is a 3/4-inch-diameter brush for each color. Large arm movements allow the brush to dance across the paper. Colors are usually chosen randomly, at least three or four on each painting. But when a strong emotion is present or has been triggered by a specific color, then that color or colors may be used exclusively until the emotional state subsides.

Despite the fact that the eight colors form a key element in CMT, do not expect this book to enlighten you on the meaning of any color. Throughout history humankind has been enthralled and influenced by color, but it refuses to reveal its mysteries. Read *Primary Colors* by Alexander Theroux (see Bibliography) — 67 pages devoted to blue, 91 to yellow, and 110 to red — and you will never again think it is possible to ascribe one meaning and one meaning only to any color.

We each see colors in our own way, and our way changes depending on the circumstance, our emotional state, our history, and in what form the color comes to us. It makes a difference whether a color is part of a piece of clothing, a road sign, the light of a heat lamp, or liquid paint coming off a brush, shining and shimmering onto the paper spread out on the work table. A favorite color for a car or clothing, when seen in a paint pot, can be surprisingly repulsive. Interestingly, this sort of response almost always changes over time. In CMT a color of paint that is repulsive at first is generally viewed later on as very desirable.

Some people approach their first painting sessions with childlike glee, daubing and splashing about with the bright colors. They find excitement in choosing and combining them. Variations of stripes, circles or zigzags cover the page. The pleasure in this activity may be expressed with singing, humming, or whistling. The session ends with the satisfaction of having had some fun.

Others approach the act of painting with apprehension. They simply cannot get into a playful mood. They have concerns about wasting time and money, doubts and uncertainties about the legitimacy of the process, resulting in sessions which produce tension, irritability and fatigue.

In the painting sessions, people may find it hard to remember to welcome *all* thoughts and emotions, no matter how depressive or aggressive they may be, and to freely express these thoughts and emotions not only with whatever colors feel appropriate to them, but also with sounds and body movements — yelling, cursing, crying, laughing,

"It is strange how deeply colors seem to penetrate, like scent."

- Dorothea Brooke in George Eliot's *Middlemarch*

swinging their arms, whacking the paper with the brush, and kicking up their heels.

After painting is finished for the day, the time spent on record keeping and reflecting on what has just happened is a very important part of the CMT session. During this after-period, being kind to oneself is essential; I highly recommend luxuriating in a hot bath, having a rest, or going for a walk. Even when the painting session has been peaceful, continuing to be alone for a while helps to prepare for a smooth reentry into "normal" consciousness. Not scheduling enough time to allow for these periods of reflection is like mixing and kneading a bread dough but never baking it.

The rules for Mess Painting, which are given in greater detail in Chapter 4, may appear maddeningly ambiguous at first; but within their structured framework they provide a safe environment for uninhibited self-expression.

After an often frustrating initial adjustment period, most Mess Painters are able to be so focused while painting that nothing else matters. Tension-building responses to the act of painting — such as fear, self-doubt or self-criticism — are no longer present. As the experience of painting becomes totally absorbing, the prevailing feeling is one of freedom and effortless control. Once learned, the method provides enough challenge to ward off boredom, but not so much challenge as to produce anxiety. It is in this middle ground between boredom and anxiety, without consciousness of "self" and with full, non-striving, very relaxed attention to the task at hand, that any activity becomes a favorable or optimal experience.

To be sure, this optimal experience is usually not present in the beginning stage of CMT, when such practical issues as setting up a functional work space, mixing the paint, and learning to handle the paper and brushes require active, concentrated attention. But once the setting-up stage is completed and the instructions can be followed automatically, without thought, one moves toward a passive state of attention where all self-consciousness has vanished. At this point, all sorts of interesting things begin to happen in daily life. Attitudes and behaviors begin to shift. Creativity blooms and is expressed in many different ways.

Benefits of CMT

The Healing Power of Creativity. In exploring the issue of what makes well people weller, or what promotes well-being, Luthe came to essentially the same conclusion that psychologist Abraham Maslow did: that creativity is the plus factor. Maslow once said that the concept of a normal, healthy, self-actualizing human being and the concept of creativity are coming closer and closer together, and may turn out to be the same thing.

The marvelous experience with color and brushwork provided by CMT brings the participant to a boundless sense of freedom that is difficult to attain in any other way. The method mobilizes energies and develops attitudes which foster creativity, allowing an openness to new ideas, new experiences, and an acceptance of non-ordinary, transcendent realities. The CMT painting process reduces fear of risk-taking and difficulties in decision-making. It assists the release of psychologically disturbing material such as aggression, anxiety, and depression, while activating the non-dominant hemisphere of the brain whose systems — visual, spatial, symbolic, holistic, and intuitive — are essential for promoting creativity.

My colleague Michael Greene, of Kansas City, Missouri, has commented:

"The power of self-regulation and self-initiated change made possible by CMT is devalued in a culture more attuned to preparing individuals for their roles as patients, clients, students, employees, churchgoers, taxpayers, and consumers, than for leading life in their own original way. The process is based on innate, individual capabilities, nurturing highly personal outcomes, and it defies the prescriptive, predictive, conventional wisdom of American medical and psychological practice. What is life-enhancing for one individual may be simply irrelevant in the life of someone else. In that paradox lies the value of CMT for all those who seek a way to ignite the creative spark that enables us, in Luthe's words, 'to become more of who we really are.'"

As my clients have added more pleasure to their lives with this painting process, so have I. I never tire of looking at the hundreds of paintings produced, listening to what happened during the painting sessions, and giving feedback on what I've seen and heard. In helping people to learn Mess Painting, I am really helping them to move closer to their authentic selves, and when this occurs it is sheer delight. In this process I am intentionally a facilitator rather than a therapist or teacher.

Mess Painting does more than provide relaxation and enjoyment. It generates the healing out of which changes in physiological and psychological functioning arise. Susan described well the healing power she discovered through mobilizing her creativity:

"I was surprised by my sense of creativity. This challenged a deeply held belief and fear about myself that I am dull and unimaginative. At some joyous moments during Mess Painting when I felt I was expressing something very true to myself, I would feel that my creative abilities were boundless. I was surprised that I felt so much passion — and delighted with how alive I felt.

"This new sense of myself was present in my life outside of painting, as well. At one point I found myself in an old familiar internal dilemma — about to relinquish something that I deeply believe in, in order to please someone close to me and to keep the peace. In the past I have mourned and berated myself for doing this. I always imagined it would take great will and courage (and feel like the climax of a Cecil B. DeMille epic) to change this pattern. In this instance, however, with a kind of deep and quiet assurance I did what was right for me; I held a Passover Seder ceremony with my young son, who wanted to participate in this ritual. I felt no fear of annihilation at his father's disapproval but rather let it be, matter of factly, as just another element in my life.

"To my surprise this has left me overall with a new feeling of inner power and strength. I feel more objective in

> *"In the west the act of creation is associated with struggle and suffering, whereas in East Asia creative people are supposed to be totally relaxed."*
>
> - Kazuaki Tanahashi

relation to others, far less subject to outside judgments, not concerned anymore with what my next sentence 'should be.' It still is so amazing to me that all of this truly new behavior could have come out of those nights of painting one painting after another after another in seemingly endless repetition."

Emotional Release. We all need to unload aggression. If we continually load a truck on one side with anger, it will get overloaded unless we unload it from the other side. (Of course, we must also make changes in our lifestyle so that we don't continue to load the truck.) CMT provides an outlet for releasing anger and aggression in privacy, so that we can handle interpersonal relations with greater equanimity rather than creating more anger and discord in the world.

"Art washes away from the soul the debris of everyday life."

- Pablo Picasso

To my great surprise I found that I am one of those who release a great deal of anger and aggression through Mess Painting. In my private painting space I can be noisy and irrational without frightening or annoying anyone else. I get great satisfaction from hearing the splat of paint on the paper and the walls — and it's much cheaper than breaking dishes!

The experience of creativity has a healing power that goes directly to each individual's needs for clearing blocks and releasing emotions. Psychotherapist Jan Berry Kadrie wrote eloquently of this aspect of CMT:

"When I entered a second CMT group in 1991, I found that even in the beginning there was little resistance. I was painting freely, and without self-criticism. I was thrilled again and again as I discovered and rediscovered that creativity is not a gift bestowed upon a chosen few nor dependent upon the intellect to figure out. Creativity is everyone's birthright.

In addition, the creativity I was finding in painting was overflowing into the rest of my life and I was experiencing a much fuller, freer, happier version of myself than ever before.

"About this time I began supervising interns who were training to become psychotherapists. I knew that CMT would help these beginning therapists develop their main instrument — themselves — and so I was soon urging them to work with Virginia for their own personal and professional development. The results were extremely positive. People in training with me reported that CMT was having impact, at the deepest levels, on their personal lives as well as on their professional work. They were discovering the amazing power of CMT to unlock memories and remove blocks. They were finding the healing power of creativity — just as I had."

Career Enhancement. CMT also sets the stage for new inventions and approaches to work, for established professional artists and non-artists alike. Jonathan Meader, whose work has been acquired by many prominent collectors and by such major museums as the Metropolitan, the Whitney, the Corcoran, and the National Gallery, decided to try CMT because of the enthusiasm of two friends who announced they were going to do it again:

"Since I'm always interested in new things, new processes, new books, new educational methods, I decided to join them. My curiosity had been heightened by seeing the documentary film on CMT. I had come to a place in my artwork where I wanted a change. Everything seemed to fit together.

"What I had not expected was that the particular kind of movements required in CMT would aggravate an injured shoulder and wrist. Eventually I had to give in to the pain and I stopped Mess Painting prematurely; however, I continued to come to the group meetings.

"I enjoyed seeing people who thought they had no art talent become very excited and delighted with the combinations of color and form they created in some of their paintings. I found what they said about the changes they were making in their lives and the paintings they produced very interesting and encouraging. We are all capable of so much more than we believe because over our

lifetimes we've learned to think of ourselves in limiting ways. CMT certainly helped people in my group take on new challenges.

"I had a couple of tremendous breakthroughs in the month following the end of the CMT group, including birthing a book that had been rolling around in my mind for years. The first painting I ever sold led to this book. This is something anyone could see if they looked at them together. However, by the time the book presented itself to my mind in a form that was complete and publishable, thirty years had gone by. I don't know just how much credit to give to CMT for this breakthrough because there were a couple of events that happened coincidentally that probably also contributed, but it certainly participated in this instantaneous invention. 'Letting go' permits surprising things to happen.

"I believe CMT played a part in the shift in my art. My fine art, which I distinguish from my posters, stage backdrops etc., has a lot of tightness. I continue to use all the same techniques that require a great deal of technical skill and my language is still precise, but instead of recognizable forms I've shifted into a more abstract expression that has a cool, intellectual quality that pleases me."

> *Jonathan Meader's* Wordless Travel Book *(Ten Speed Press, 1996), created following his CMT experience, is designed to allow travelers abroad to make their needs known without having to speak an unfamiliar language. They simply point at pictures, arranged by categories.*

Behavioral Change. Many of my clients report caring less about what other people think of them well before their CMT program has ended, and most of them make noticeable, self-fulfilling, self-affirming behavioral changes during the seven weeks of CMT and during the following months — *not the least of which is having more fun.* Increasing the amount of gaiety in one's life is no small accomplishment. Remember Norman Cousins, who laughed himself well from a normally fatal illness, and concluded: *"Your very life depends upon having a good time."*

On occasion a person considering CMT tells me about a particular emotional reaction that he or she would like to be rid of. When Emily, a gentle, soft-spoken woman of eighty-two, called about joining a CMT group, she revealed that tears would well up and often overflow if she received any kindly attention — a gift, a favor, a compliment, or a physical expression of affection. She felt that her inability to control her tears was inappropriate behavior and evidence of weakness. It made her feel embarrassed, vulnerable, and inadequate in social and familial situations.

I welcomed her as a participant but did not give her any reassurance that CMT would decrease her unwanted crying. I simply told her that something interesting would probably transpire during her involvement with this work.

After an average amount of difficulty, Emily became comfortable with the process and looked forward to her painting sessions. The three other women in her group were thirty to forty years younger than Emily. Two of them were dealing with serious family problems and found in Mess Painting a powerful tool to activate the catharsis they needed for their anger and grief. Their responses to CMT made Emily think she should be reviewing her disappointing marriage, which had ended in divorce thirty years before. I intervened, suggesting that she need not actively dredge up old history; she could just wait and see what memories chose to surface.

With permission to trust her own reactions, Emily relaxed. She enjoyed using the tempera paint, a medium she had not touched since her college days when drawing and painting had been her minor area of study. Her painting became more spontaneous and she laughed at the surprising results. Toward the end of each session after the Mess Painting period was over, she began to explore how she could paint mountains, skies, clouds, trees, leaves, and blossoms authentically. She didn't want objects to appear too real, just identifiable. (See Illustration 1, page 129.)

At our final meeting, calm and self-confident, Emily shared a letter from her college art professor complimenting her work — a letter she had kept safely hidden for sixty-one years. When it was her turn at the final meeting to see a few of her own favorite Mess Paintings placed, one after another, behind glass in a handsome gold frame, Emily listened, dry-eyed, to everyone's praise. The following Christmas I received a letter from her:

"Dear Virginia:

"My life is working for me. Because of Mess Painting, my responses to relatives changed. I have been able to say directly, 'Please don't take away my independence. I need to make this decision more slowly on my own.' And with friends and neighbors, instead of always saying, 'All right' or 'Surely, if you want to' or 'If that's the way you prefer,' I now say, 'Can we do that Thursday or Friday afternoon instead of today? I would prefer to finish what I am doing now.'

"P.S. I realize I have not mentioned the tears — they seem so relatively unimportant. Could my embarrassment have been dispelled so quickly?"

Physical Healing. Many people come to CMT with some unspoken problem, such as excessive perspiring, improper bowel function, or insomnia. Such complaints are generally not mentioned to me in the beginning, probably partly because most people don't expect painting — any sort of painting — to be of help with these sorts of problems.

"Letting go" with paint may surprisingly bring some relief or even complete resolution of a physical problem. Given the right conditions, our inner healer appears to be capable of restoring a healthy balance unless some further abuse interferes. Clients of mine have been astonished when a physical ailment improved or vanished when the only new element in their life was CMT. A nursery school teacher reported improvement in a physical problem after only three weeks of CMT. At the fourth meeting of her group she marched in declaring, *"Mess Painting is marvelous. I'm having the most wonderful poops. I don't need Metamucil anymore."* The other women chuckled at her announcement, and one shyly added, *"That's happening to me too, but I didn't connect it to Mess Painting."*

Henry tells the following story of his physical healing in my film about CMT: *"I've been doing Mess Painting, with short vacations from it, for almost a year now. I enjoy the sensuous and soothing feelings as the brush seems to move by itself over the paper. After the first several weeks my excessive perspiring and salivating stopped and chronic colitis abated. Possibilities of realizing inner harmony opened up."*

Creative Solutions to Ordinary Dilemmas. Besides physical healing, Henry found that CMT offered a creative solution to his difficulty with absorbing new information:

"I changed occupations five years ago and was unable to study and keep up with new developments. I had gone into more and more self-coercive attempts to study, with no success. A couple of months ago I tried using a CMT approach. I would go over formidable material quickly and superficially, instead of trying desperately to grasp it for the first time. I whistled and hummed and did problems carelessly, not caring if I got them right. This procedure conformed to CMT and violated traditional strict 'whole attention' methods. In a couple of weeks a technical book that had been my enemy became my friend. Who would guess that Mess Painting would lead to such an unexpected result?"

Enriched Sensory Awareness. For everyone engaging in CMT, there is in addition an unexpected gift of increased visual awareness and sensitivity. One CMT painter wrote:

"One day after painting when I left my work space in the garage and walked through the garden I stood absolutely transfixed by the beauty of droplets of water hanging on blades of grass. At that moment nothing else existed; I was one with the universe." Another described seeing a pattern of mold on an apartment house step so fascinating it was worthy of a long five-minute stare. And many CMT painters have remarked upon experiencing intensified pleasure when they attend art exhibitions.

Most of us can appreciate how Mess Painting can increase visual sensitivity — but you may be surprised to discover that CMT can also stimulate other sense modalities, such as hearing and movement. The painting technique is highly kinesthetic, and many of its benefits may stem from this fact.

Experiencing Non-Ordinary Realities. Beyond the physical senses, there is another realm accessible through CMT — a peaceful, joyous space of no-thought, which Gay Luce eloquently describes in my documentary film:

"While splashing about with the bright colors it is often irresistible to whistle, sing, dance, and enjoy happy memories. These experiences may give way, as they did for me, to mental silence and a mystical sense of the underlying unity of self and universe. In some painting sessions I would feel like I had been launched from a rocket into a place of great space and lightness . . . and as I finished painting I saw the world as though veils had been lifted from my eyes."

Gay's remarkably beautiful paintings, which accompany her narration, are a high point of the film (See Illustration 12, page 132).

Changes in Relationships. When the behavior of one member of a family markedly changes, it may alter the dynamics between that person and each of the other members, and/or have a ripple effect producing changes in their attitudes or behavior.

It has been fascinating to me to observe how quickly children understand the value of having parents Mess Paint. Coming home from school and finding Mother in a bad mood will prompt children to ask, "Have you painted today?" One of the delights for a parent involved with this painting process is having a college-bound son or daughter demand that a particular painting be framed so they can hang it in their room at school.

Jo, an energetic mother and high school drama teacher, wrote mostly about her relationship with her family in her final summary of her CMT experience:

"I wondered how on earth I would have time to do CMT, do my job, be mother and wife all at the same time. I trusted that somehow I could manage it. What I found out is that not only did I 'manage' it just fine, but the time taken for myself did not take away from my work or family one bit: it added to it! During the weeks of CMT I miraculously found time to make curtains for Erica's room, and I offered meals to my family which I cooked as gifts — enjoying the creativity, care and nurturing that went into them for my family, rather than resenting

having to do them because 'no one else will.' CMT helped me to see that life is bigger than the roles I feel obligated to fill successfully as a mother, wife, house-keeper, cook, productive employee, dedicated parent volunteer and so on.

"There has been more harmony, more acceptance, more support and general good feelings in my family since I started CMT. What I do in my own space (my husband calls it my 'simulated padded cell') has made me more respectful and accepting of my husband's own need and desire for privacy and 'messing.' Now I'm much less judgmental and intolerant when he is 'playing' and not 'producing.' His support, enthusiasm, encouragement and respect for my privacy and my process during this CMT course have deepened my love and respect and appreciation for him, and have provided a model for me to follow. I have also been more accessible — open, spontaneous and accepting — with my high school students."

In describing her ten-year-old daughter's response to her Mess Paint-ings and to art in general, Jo reported that her daughter had hated abstract art, and couldn't understand the value of anything that wasn't at least trying to look like something real. From the beginning of Jo's involvement in CMT, however, Erica seemed to understand on an intuitive level the value and beauty of her mother's efforts and of the process of "messing." Erica's own art work became much freer, and she asked her mother to take her to galleries and museums to see as much modern art as possible. Throughout the two months of CMT her attitude toward her mother's art and work was totally support-ive. On more than one occasion she made the unsolicited observation, "Mess Painting is really good for you. You're a lot better, Mom." Jo's response had been to laugh to herself and think, "Of course! I'm less focused on her. What a relief this must be for her. It certainly is for me."

Jo had an unanticipated short visit from her mother and father while she was involved with CMT, and she told me:

"The painting I did while my parents were visiting felt like just what I've needed to do to get back on center when I go off, as I do so easily when we are together. Although I didn't paint as much as I'd have liked during that time, I finally understood the need to take time for myself and to stay engaged in my own interests no matter what is happening around me."

Having her parents in the house was obviously a good test for Jo, but it was the dialogues with phantom "others," including her parents, that she carried on while painting that helped prepare her to be more honest, assertive, and congruent in her interactions with others, including her brother.

CMT does involve some risks. When someone does Mess Painting in a household shared with others, it may contribute to a reappraisal of relationships — depending on the cooperation or interference of roommates or family members. This may result in a decision to move out and live under conditions where one can express oneself more freely and enjoy greater harmony with oneself and others.

Producing Fascinating Paintings. Although this is emphatically not the goal of this process-oriented endeavor, you will find at the end of your program that you have created a number of wonderful paintings, some of which you will want to frame for display in your home. These paintings are as much a part of you as any of the others, and you will likely take pleasure in embracing the beauty and intensity that has been able to manifest itself when you learned to let your conscious, critical, goal-driven mind get out of the way.

Kathy Goss wrote in her final review:

"I began Mess Painting with some apprehension. I was afraid that I couldn't paint and couldn't draw. Having permission to paint freely, with no concern for the product, allowed me to break through my performance anxiety.

"During the first week I was astonished at how much beauty was coming out of me in the paintings. I felt joyful, and had a surprising feeling of competence.

"I was even more surprised at the group meetings when the others obviously enjoyed my paintings, especially the unusual marbling effects and ghostlike images that had appeared on the paper quite by accident.

"In the fourth week I did a number of desert landscapes at the end of my Mess Painting sessions. This was a tremendous breakthrough, since I had avoided trying to paint anything 'real' out of fear that I couldn't. I took great pleasure in

creating these paintings, which evoked for me the feeling of special remembered desert places. And, amazingly, the members of the group not only admired the paintings, but even seemed to respond to their deeply personal emotional content.

"Mess Painting not only brought me new insights and the release of long-contained emotions, but it also introduced me to a new medium for expressing my feelings to others. As a professional communicator — poet, musician, and prose writer — I felt validated and empowered to discover that I could also communicate effectively through painting."

Henry Miller would have completely understood Kathy's delight in finding another way to express feelings. In his book on painting he states: *"When one is an artist* [meaning writer, painter, musician, actor, etc.] *. . . all mediums open up. For no one medium is sufficient to express the wealth of feeling which burdens the soul of an artist."*

How Important is Group Support in Doing CMT?

CMT groups meeting without a trained facilitator have not been successful. Confusion and arguments caused the groups to fall apart and discouraged the members from continuing by themselves.

Doing CMT sessions under guidance on an individual basis has proven to have certain advantages. People can proceed more slowly if that is appropriate, and can continue with CMT for as long as they wish or need. On the other hand, meeting in a group with a facilitator can provide support. Seeing how each member struggles with essentially the same life issues can reinforce a sense of community, as well as a respect for individual uniqueness. But the amount of bonding that takes place varies greatly from group to group.

One woman I worked with found herself in a group where the other members wanted to analyze everything, and although I intervened she heard enough to feel criticized. This dampened her pleasure in the painting process. Writer Katy Butler, on the other hand, felt quite indifferent to the group. She liked the fact that *"CMT is a self-healing process. You go to the group meeting and you see everybody's work. You are encouraged to continue and given a little direction, but essentially it's the process of getting in touch with your own body, your own deeper self, and this happens at home."*

Another group participant said his experience would have been greatly improved if the rest of the group had been more involved, done more paintings, participated more, and been more self-disclosing. He felt exposed when he shared and others did not. Another complained about others being absent or arriving unprepared and having to organize their paintings at the meetings. Especially in a CMT group, members need to keep up the pace of painting four sessions each week. It can be demoralizing in a small group to have one or more participants arrive at the weekly meeting with only one or two sessions of paintings.

Because Mess Painting was designed by Luthe to be done at home in solitude, it is particularly well suited to a self-help approach. I strongly advise interested readers who live in areas where there are no certified CMT facilitators to accept the challenge of working on their own. And some CMT participants have found the process so satisfying that they have kept their painting setup permanently so that they can continue to do more Mess Painting from time to time.

Who Should Do CMT?

As I pointed out earlier, CMT is at its best when it is part of a "well" person's journey toward individuation. Secretaries and psychiatrists, nurses, housewives and house-husbands, psychotherapists, gardeners, acupuncturists, teachers, carpenters, civil servants, chiropractors, technicians, lawyers, artists, writers, musicians, and even a priest have all put more fun and freedom in their lives with CMT. So have students in a variety of fields — art, creative writing, dance, music, art therapy, electronics, psychology, nursing, and occupational therapy.

CMT is every bit as appropriate for people who have little or no experience with art materials as it is for professional artists who need a booster shot to revitalize their creativity. For both artists and non-artists, the psychological and physiological changes that come about from engaging in this painting process are varied, and reflect the differences among individuals.

However, the method is not appropriate for everyone who might wish to explore it. It is not advised, for example, for borderline personality disorders, for anyone who has had psychotic episodes, for those unable or unwilling to follow the instructions, and for most drug abusers.

Only once in over twenty years have I had to ask someone to stop Mess Painting — a young man who demonstrated that he was unable to follow instructions. During the two weeks he was part of a group he applied the paint only in the center area of the paper, and this congested area looked like scrambled brains. The appearance of the paintings and his inability to describe what went on while he painted led me to suspect he was a heavy drug user. He acknowledged that he used drugs, and I referred him to a treatment center.

While I would not knowingly accept someone into a CMT group who was on drugs, there was one instance where the outcome was positive. The young woman in question, the highly regarded office manager of a law firm, smoked a small amount of marijuana on a daily basis. This habit had kept her from reading, taking classes, and carrying out ideas for art projects. I learned this piece of her history only after her CMT group had ended and she was working with me individually. She explained that she had stopped smoking pot after five weeks of Mess Painting, and that she needed to paint and see me until she felt she could stay clean. After a month or so she discontinued Mess Painting and began developing her artistic skills, working with clay as her preferred medium. From then on she could confidently say, *"I credit CMT with helping me quit a fifteen-year marijuana addiction."*

When she joined another CMT group about three years later, she had already had two exhibits of her art work. This time she hoped for and found more self-confidence in handling love relationships. She was married a year later.

If you are currently in therapy, you can do CMT at the same time. Possibly one-third or more of the people I have worked with were seeing a psychotherapist while doing CMT. I suggest that you show this book to your therapist before starting CMT on your own.

CMT participants know they may telephone me if they need to. But in more than twenty years of working with this painting process, it has been extremely rare that someone would call because they were seriously frightened or overwhelmed by a flood of emotion while painting. Instead of uncontrollable emotional outbursts, the opposite problem has prevailed. Most people attracted to CMT have blocks to "letting go" and barriers to being playful. The procedures and strategies of the CMT technique have enabled almost everyone to overcome these impediments, which are often the result of childhood learning experiences.

How to Use This Book

If You Are Interested in Doing Mess Painting. If you accept my invitation to have an adventure by painting your way to desirable changes in your life, and assuming that you do not fall into any of the categories of people for whom I have said CMT may not be advisable, ask yourself at a gut level whether you are willing to commit the seven weeks needed for the program, and if you can find a suitable work space for this activity.

If you have done this and are prepared to commit the time and resources necessary for a CMT program, please read this entire book carefully before purchasing your supplies. To make shopping easier I have provided detailed descriptions of the materials and equipment needed and a checklist to copy and take along. I also give precise guidance for setting up your work space.

My instructions on how to proceed through the steps of the program include guidelines as to what you may expect as you move from the frustrations of the early painting sessions into the later phases of CMT. The book contains exercises and a list of suggested readings to help you overcome resistance and enrich your experience. Be sure to read this additional material if you run into difficulties.

Finally, for those who find they need extra support, details are provided in the Epilogue about contacting me to make a financial arrangement to receive my guidance by correspondence.

If You Are Not a Candidate for CMT. Perhaps you are reading this book just to understand what the Creativity Mobilization Technique is all about. I think the book, describing as it does the great variety of responses to CMT, can be enlightening and entertaining even if you are not a candidate for the program. Besides, after reading *The Magic of Mess Painting* you may think of just the friend or family member for whom it would be an exciting and valuable gift.

---

[1]Linda Sonrisa and Toby Rowland-Jones, in *Ping-Pong*, Journal of the Henry Miller Library, Big Sur, CA, 1(2):1996, p. 46.

[2]Marcia Pear, *What you Need to Know - a Road Map for Personal Transformation.* See Bibliography for additional information.

[3] Gay Luce is currently founding director and instructor at the Nine Gates Mystery School, which gives students experiences of ancient rites of initiation into spiritual enlightenment and wisdom teachings.

Chapter 2

Letting Go

"Our general failure (over the past three thousand years of human history) to notice the inseparability of things, and to be aware of our own basic unity with the external world, is the result of specializing in a particular kind of consciousness. For we have very largely based culture and civilization on concentrated attention, on using the mind as a spotlight rather than a floodlight, and by this means analyzing the world into separate bits. Concentrated attention is drummed into us in schools; it is essential to the three R's; it is the foundation of all careful thought and detailed description. . . But the price we pay for this vision of the world in vivid detail, bit by bit, is that we lose sight of the relationships and unities between the bits."

- Humphry Osmond

"No-Thought" Mess Painting is a unique experience. There is little to learn in a formal way. Rather what is necessary is to shift out of the tension we usually feel when learning something new — to let go into a relaxed state of being in which we are open to whatever comes. This is the state known as "flow" or "optimal experience."

Optimal experience is nothing new. We have all known it as young children. Preschoolers move effortlessly from one thing to another, each activity claiming their full attention, but without the tension that we adults have come to associate with being fully focused on something. As youngsters explore their worlds, their ability to be one with whatever they are doing is enviable. This kind of experience is an end in itself; it is not "good" in an absolute sense. It is valuable in that it has the potential to make life more intense and meaningful, and because it increases the strength of the self. When people are able to shift easily into this state of consciousness and do so frequently, they feel that their existence has meaning and their lives are worth living.

For most adults this shift is not easy to make. I believe that much of the difficulty stems from all the do's, don'ts and threats most of us heard in childhood from parents, older siblings, teachers, and other adults. Such injunctions, almost always negative and seldom uttered in a loving tone of voice, are unfortunately considered an essential part of child rearing, repeated from generation to generation. These negative messages bolster conformity at the expense of self-esteem and creativity. This old, outdated model of child-rearing is particularly unhelpful today, when the freedom to act intuitively and autonomously is so crucial to survival in our rapidly changing world.

Psychologist Stanley Krippner, who has a keen interest in what helps or hinders the development of creativity, summarized some of these negative admonitions in what he calls "The Ten Commandments that Interfere with Creativity."

THE TEN COMMANDMENTS THAT INTERFERE WITH CREATIVITY

I. *Thou Shalt Not Rock The Cultural Boat.*
II. *Everything Thou Doest Must be Useful.*
III. *Everything Thou Doest Must Be Successful.*
IV. *Everything Thou Doest Must Be Perfect.*
V. *Everyone Thou Knowest Must Like Thee.*
VI. *Thou Shalt Not Diverge From Culturally Imposed Gender Norms.*
VII. *Thou Shalt Not Prefer Solitude To Togetherness.*
VIII. *Thou Shalt Not Be Ambiguous.*
IX. *Remember Concentrated Attention And Keep It Holy.*
X. *Thou Shalt Not Express Excessive Emotional Feeling.*
- Stanley Krippner

To some degree we are all captives of what we were so easily led to believe as children. Even the most self-aware of my Mess Painting students — often the graduates of extensive therapy — discover that they are still influenced and inhibited by early programming. Messing around, playing with the paint, and being irrational are an important part of CMT — yet many adults do not feel free to explore such possibilities.

One woman, describing the benefits she had realized from CMT, said: *"Another wonderful awareness that came after I began to make more of a 'fool' of myself, to give myself more permission, was discovering or beginning to discover the child in me, sensing sometimes what play really is, how non-directed and utterly whimsical and in-the-moment it is."*

That description recalled my own experience with CMT, and I could fully appreciate her surprise and delight. On the other hand, I have worked with people whose childhoods contained far greater emotional and physical pain than anything I personally experienced. Although I could not "know" what they had gone through in the same way, I would feel profound awe at their ability to use CMT to help heal their truly dreadful psychic wounds.

Letting Go of Practicality

The American emphasis on practicality has produced many worthwhile results, but it can be carried too far. As I began to share my enthusiasm about CMT with others and introduce it into my work, I naturally expected to meet resistance to the idea that making a mess with paint and brush could be worthwhile. But the resistance I have encountered has been far greater than I anticipated. I believe this resistance stems from a deeply ingrained idea that everything we do must be useful.

Hoping to seduce the devotees of practicality into exploring the irrationality of Mess Painting, in 1978 I created my documentary film about CMT. I was lucky to have in one of my groups at that time an older woman, Iris, who had decided to try Mess Painting in the hope that it would help her get back to her delicate collage work, which she had not been doing for some time. I thought her particular difficulties with letting go, and her ultimate success with Mess Painting, would fit my purpose beautifully.

Iris readily agreed to appear in the film, and wrote an accurate and entertaining script about the remarkable experiences she had had with CMT. She delivered her script on film without hesitation in her clear, crisp English accent:

"Frankly, there were times when I decided CMT was a total rip-off. I am by nature orderly; I don't function well in a mess. It angered me to leave routine jobs undone in order to slap paint onto newspaper. It seemed like a shocking waste of time, energy, and money, aimlessly making the same strokes, producing the same muddy daubings day after day. Gloom set in."

At this point in her encounter with CMT, Iris' paintings were somewhat messy but they were not Mess Paintings. They had not been done in a state of passive concentration with an open mind. While she painted, Iris' critical, judgmental faculties were kept busy full time, commenting negatively on what she was doing. She had not developed a casual indifference to what was appearing on the paper. Fortunately she persisted, despite her considerable misgivings. Eventually the process took over, and she was able to let go.

During one of the weekly meetings, I noticed in some half-dozen of Iris' paintings a similar, barely discernible shape near the center. It looked like a weird, perhaps bandaged, head. When I pointed to the repetition of this shape, Iris was astonished. She had not noticed it before, but she immediately acknowledged it as something very familiar: *"I recognized that head as the almost featureless, yet venomously threatening, blob that has haunted my dreams for years. It appears very suddenly, sometimes even in my happiest dreams. I have never been able to describe or discuss what was so terrifying about it that I would awake screaming in fear."*

Iris and I could have speculated that the grim head might be related to what she had seen during her years of driving an ambulance in London during World War II, or heaven knows what else; but with CMT such probing into the painter's history is neither appropriate nor necessary. After a further period of very dark Mess Paintings, the menacing blob lost its power to frighten

Iris and then disappeared from her dreams.

Iris had another positive and unexpected outcome which she divulged in the film: *"I had driven a car frequently, fearlessly, and accident-free for many years, but fourteen years ago when I came to this country from the British Isles I developed a fear of driving that has never left me — until now!"*

Iris had hoped that Mess Painting would remove the block that was keeping her from her art work. Within a few months after the group ended, she had completed enough collages for an exhibition at a local bank. That alone would have been a more than acceptable result. Certainly neither Iris nor I could have predicted that she would also banish a recurring nightmare and recover from a phobia so easily.

I have also seen CMT help people recover from their fear of flying. Veronica had a mild flying phobia which diminished the pleasure of accompanying her husband, a collector of modern art, on trips around the country and abroad. Through Mess Painting she got in touch with her early childhood experience of traveling with her family over the open waters between the San Juan Islands in an unsteady, rocking boat. Once she was able to reexperience her childhood terror of these boat trips, her queasiness about air travel vanished.

Releasing Success and Perfection Hangups

Our achievement-oriented culture promotes the idea that we should be thoroughly competent and adequate in whatever we do. I believe that children steeped in this tradition hide their imaginative thoughts for fear of ridicule and censure; then when they become adults, doubtful that they can realize their inventive ideas, they keep them closeted. I believe that admonitions to "be successful" and to "do everything perfectly" set up lifelong inner voices that tell people they are not smart enough, attractive enough, or good enough for the jobs, courses of study, hobbies, relationships, and social roles they desire.

Many success-oriented people have worked so hard to excel in their profession or business that they have no time left for enjoying life. Yet they continue this self-destructive pattern because they don't feel satisfied or secure about what they have attained. They don't know how to be purposeless, to just "hang out" or "be in the now."

For Judy, a Rosen Method massage student, Mess Painting brought an insight about her success syndrome: *"I feel like the way I paint now (in my CMT sessions) has become a metaphor for the way I'm starting to live my life. I got real clear during early painting sessions that I have a very strong need to be in control. I could see so strongly my paralysis around becoming myself. I felt the parental injunctions of 'Do it right' and 'Look good' were living my life for me. I also became very aware of how important it was for me to always be special, outstanding, extraordinary, and how my attachment to these needs ran my life."*

There is certainly nothing wrong with being successful, but the very desire for success may create anxiety and actually interfere with achieving good results. Generally speaking, truly successful people — from surgeons to auto mechanics — like what they do so much that their absorption in the task overrides concerns about how well they are doing it. Such people often remark that they sometimes feel a bit guilty about the money they earn, because they find their work so enjoyable.

It is not easy to ignore internalized injunctions to be perfect. We have all heard someone say, "Anything worth doing is worth doing well," which we all too often understand to mean "perfectly." The paradox of doing a Mess Painting "perfectly" certainly has its humor. But faced with the task of learning something new, even something like Mess Painting, people tend to be very serious. I have great difficulty getting across the idea that the paintings people produce while learning to let go *are all worth doing.*

Eventually in CMT almost everyone gets rid of at least some of their success and perfection hangups, although the time it takes varies greatly among individuals. Once they are swinging along with the painting process, this compulsion may simply disappear, as it did for two women pianists I worked with, who had both given up their music after failing to achieve the artistic success they sought. Phyllis and June grew up in different cities, were different ages, learned to Mess Paint years apart, and never met; but both had pursued the goal of being a concert pianist, and when that didn't work out, had abandoned playing the piano. Without constant practice, they would strike occasional wrong notes, which they found unbearable, depriving them of any pleasure in playing. Neither had played the piano at all in ten years or more. Phyllis was now in her thirties, had never married, and had pursued a career as a dental assistant; June was in her forties with teenaged daughters, and worked as a teacher and art therapist in a school for the handicapped.

Phyllis did CMT for seven weeks, and June for nine weeks. The experience enabled both women to overcome an excessive need for perfection and to enjoy making music again. Whether playing the works of their favorite composers or improvising, they discovered they could happily perform for friends without fear, and without caring if they made a few mistakes.

Incapacitating performance anxiety can arise from parental admonitions in childhood about perfection and success. Probably the most dramatic example I have seen of a cure of stage fright through Mess Painting was the one achieved by Carl, a violinist. He was referred to me by his psychiatrist, who thought that an essentially non-verbal process like CMT would be a valuable addition to Carl's treatment. We decided that individual work would meet his needs better than being in a time-limited group, since he would probably need to continue painting far beyond the usual two-month period.

An anxious appearing man in his mid-sixties, Carl had received cruel and unusual treatment from his father and little love from a mother who had never once come to his rescue. The father, having conceived the idea that his son should become a famous violinist like Menuhin, insisted the boy practice every day and not play outside after school with other children. To force him to practice long hours the father, screaming and cursing, frequently threatened him with a butcher knife. As a child and teenager, Carl had often awakened in the middle of the night to find his father standing by his bed cursing him for not practicing enough, saying over and over, "You're no damn good! You ungrateful bastard!"

Carl did become a professional musician, but not in the concert halls of his father's dreams: he played in large dance bands. However, his stage fright was so pervasive that he could never perform without a few drinks. As the years went by his alcoholism increased. He began having blackouts, he was fired from jobs, lost contact with his wife and children, and finally became a derelict.

With hospitalization, follow-up treatment at a city clinic, attendance at AA, and help from the State Department of Rehabilitation, Carl got a menial job repairing appliances, working long hours in a dark, tiny back room where he did not meet the public. This work provided a livelihood and enabled Carl to get off welfare, but it did not utilize his talents or his considerable intelligence, and he remained extremely depressed. AA meetings were his only social outlet; they were effective for his drinking problem, but were not alleviating his emotional pain.

Carl faithfully did his four CMT sessions a week, following all my instructions. Painting with black and red called forth the rage, despair, and fear that he had never had any help with as a child. As he slapped massive amounts of these colors onto the paper day after day, he found himself reliving brutal childhood scenes with his father. As this process continued he often imagined himself turning on his father and being the victor in a violent struggle.

After eight weeks or so of painting, Carl began to enjoy all the colors as his need for catharsis diminished. Now he began to apply the underlying principles of CMT to create his own music messing exercises. His inventions were aimed specifically at overcoming his fear of making mistakes while performing.

First, as he improvised a musical mess on the piano, Carl would record it on an audio cassette. As he listened to this tape again and again, his goal was to maintain both a very relaxed body and a calm mind, free of self-criticism. His psychiatrist and I had separate opportunities to listen to the tape with Carl. We both thought his unstructured composition was similar to some new music we had heard, and told him so.

A month or so later, and for the first time in years, Carl picked up his violin. As he practiced, he recorded himself playing some popular pieces. Every now and then he would deliberately make sour, screeching sounds. For the next few weeks he spent some time each day lying on his couch, passively concentrating on relaxing his body as he listened to his violin mess music on a cassette player.

Next, Carl collected photographs — full-size portraits of people. He cut them out, glued them to cardboard and fastened them to the backs of chairs, broom handles, and what not. After arranging the pictures in front of him he played his violin, deliberately making errors as he looked into the eyes of his cardboard audience. All the while, he kept checking in on his body's state of relaxation. An added beauty in all of this activity was the fact that Carl had exercised his own inventiveness rather than just carrying out someone else's ideas.

During the next few months Carl's self-esteem grew. Now that he was spending time with his violin he no longer did any painting. I met with him infrequently, and only when he requested a session. Before long he decided to apply for work as a violinist, and was accepted for a one-night-a-week job with a small combo.

At first Carl was somewhat anxious, but he managed to enter a state of passive concentration and allow the music to play itself. Earning money as a musician increased his self-confidence, and he began to talk and joke with the other musicians between sets, something he had never been able to do before.

About two years after he started CMT, Carl was working regularly in large dance bands. During the intermissions, very erect, violin in hand, he would go down among the tables and offer to play requests. He carried a card in the pocket of his tuxedo jacket on which he had listed titles of songs for people to select from, in case they couldn't decide what they would like to hear. This solo work was his greatest joy.

I have written at length about Carl because I would like readers who are therapists to see that CMT can fit into the treatment of persons too anxious and psychologically disturbed to do CMT either on their own or in a group led by a qualified facilitator. Carl's psychiatrist and I were in good rapport, and Carl benefited from continuing to see him while he was also working with me. Therapists who have enjoyed CMT for their own growth have taken the time to become CMT facilitators, and find adding CMT to their treatment program with appropriate individuals very valuable for accelerating the treatment process. Others, like Carl's psychiatrist, prefer to encourage appropriate clients to use a guided CMT program as an adjunctive therapy.

Embracing Solitude

The fear of solitude can be another impediment to doing CMT. In part this fear arises from the challenge of giving up our obsessive need for outside stimuli, such as radio and TV, since the only sounds permissible in the CMT work space are those produced by the painter. My younger clients often object to this instruction; yet later, after the seven weeks of painting sessions have ended, they are pleased to discover that, having experienced solitude while painting, they now enjoy times alone without any rock or other background music. They are sometimes quite content to be in silence.

Another expression of the fear of solitude is a reluctance to try to learn something new without a teacher standing by ready to give advice. Our society tends to overemphasize group interaction and group dynamics. The value of constantly being with others is never questioned in educating the young. Indeed, a preference for solitude is often considered a sign of emotional instability. But there is a great difference between healthy solitude and morbid withdrawal.

Hansi, an excellent athlete and counselor-in-training, learned the value of solitude through CMT: *"The first change that occurred was the realization of my own need for solitude. I tend to fill up my time with busyness. I do have time for solitude and I created that for myself during these eight weeks. Doing the paintings showed me the door to that solitude and I walked through it. I 'get' to have that solitude now. It's my just dessert. I take long walks by myself, I work in the garden, I spend time on projects at home that allow me to be with myself, and I decline many social invitations. This solitude gives me the space, the opening, to experience what I have inside."*

Many others discover in CMT a good excuse for absenting themselves from their family or housemates. I am reminded of Anne, who had the courage to take over the family's guest bedroom for CMT. Not only had the guest room usually been full of relatives or friends, but the rest of the house tended to be packed with people as well. Anne's husband had seen to it that there were plenty of visitors, as well as the overnight guests, by scheduling frequent union and political meetings at their home in the evenings. Turning the guest room into her Mess Painting studio gave Anne the first private space she had ever possessed. She had always shared a bedroom with a sibling while growing up, had lived in a dormitory at college, had married at graduation and had shared a bedroom with her husband from then on. Since she worked full time, ridding herself of house guests was the one way to ensure having enough time for painting. Fortunately, after Anne's CMT experience, her husband was easily persuaded to add another room onto the house, for her sole use.

Tolerating Ambiguity

Another cultural taboo is the prejudice against ambiguity: *"Make up your mind!" "You can't have your cake and eat it too!"* This kind of admonition is especially hard on creative children, who can easily see advantages in all the alternatives open to them in a situation. Unfortunately adults tend to force such children into a hasty choice, rather than tolerate their tentativeness and allow all the time it may take to make a decision.

This kind of upbringing tends to create rigid people who are uncomfortable with shades of gray. They want everything to be exact — black or white, right or wrong — and when attempting Mess Painting they may become hostile because of the ambiguity inherent in the instructions and in the process. As their guide in CMT, I often get the blame for their distress; I have been the recipient of considerable animosity on this score.

An ability to tolerate ambiguity seems to be an essential element of the creative process. A willingness to allow an artistic solution to emerge during the actual act of creating the art work has been described as "problem finding" in research on creativity.

> "Some individuals, like the copyist in art, the technician in science, the pedant in scholarship, the bureaucrat in government, deal with problems that have already been identified. The fine artist, the inventive scientist, the creative scholar, the innovative statesman, the self-actualizing person are in addition aware of unformulated problems potentially present in the conflicts of their own experience; unlike machines, they devise their own programs and work on _discovered problems_.
>
> "This ability is not based on a quantitative superiority in memory, reasoning, or conventional cognitive capacities. The ability to formulate problems seems to be a faculty of a different order. It entails a process far more in touch with the deeper layers of being than reason alone usually is; it is far more holistic in that it encompasses the person's total experiential state. The process is goal-directed, but it often pursues goals beneath the threshold of awareness. It seeks out similarities between external objects and internal states; it uses symbolic means to express formless feelings, thereby disclosing that which otherwise would go unperceived, articulating what otherwise would remain unarticulated. Problem finding may well be at the origin of the creative vision."
>
> — Mihalyi Csikszentmihalyi

Expressing Emotion

The idea that one must behave in such a way as to elicit admiration and approval is instilled in children at an early age. Fear of being unloved prevents youngsters from building independence and self-respect, and can prove harmful as they grow up. It is one of the reasons adolescents forfeit their individual creative abilities for the sake of being accepted as "one of the gang."

The need for others' approval is a barrier to even appropriate expressions of emotions such as anger, which in turn blocks true intimacy in relationships. Indeed, the expression of "excessive" emotional feeling is perhaps the biggest cultural taboo of all. Many of my clients have found in Mess Painting the first safe place they have had in their lives to express anger.

For Daisy, a young art student, Mess Painting was her first opportunity to let go with her anger: *"Then I got really mad. I tore paper, yelled, got very physical and made the image I had always been afraid to make — a vagina with hands ripping at it. I was so enraged, I ended up beating up some clay I had in my work space, and throwing it against the floor. Eventually, after I had gotten through being physical with the clay, I made masks with the pieces I had thrown. I realized later that they are my mom, dad, and me."*

And Maureen wrote in her final summary: *"The course began with me getting in touch with anger immediately and that led to using two gallons and one quart of red paint! Therapists had always said I needed to express my anger and I had such a problem with that. My father had raged all the time and it never changed to anything else. In Mess Painting at first the sessions would stay in anger and depression and not change, and then to my surprise it changed and I changed. This course showed me that things, feelings, images do change and I don't have to be stuck in one emotion or denial of it. It was very exciting when that happened. There was such a range in the paintings from very angry, very depressed, catatonic, to elation, ecstasy, and freedom."*

There is such a variety of ways to respond to situations, yet most of us are stuck with one or two responses which have become habitual and which often are not in our best interest. Mess Painting offers an opportunity, as Maureen and others have discovered, to get unstuck from these habitual responses and find better ones.

My first husband, Varda, was a master of inventive responses. I was always very impressed by his reactions to situations that would make most people angry. Varda had a succession of old cars with problematical insides, and usually did not drive very fast. One day we were driving on the freeway, and Varda was telling me an interesting story about a friend of his whom I had just met. Focused on his story, as he exited he inadvertently cut across the path of a large Cadillac. As Varda pulled up at a stop sign, the Cadillac pulled up beside him, its driver yelling angrily, "You son of a bitch! You're a terrible driver!" Varda, perfectly calm, turned to the man and smiled. "Yes," he said, "you are quite right. But you'd be amazed at how good I am at other things." He drove off, leaving the other driver sputtering, and serenely continued his story.

Storytelling can be a powerful tool for healing — for the storyteller as well as the listener. Stories can demonstrate unusual ways of solving problems; they can enlarge our concepts of what is possible and help to change old attitudes and beliefs that are no longer in our best interest. For these reasons and more, storytelling is a large part of my work with people doing CMT.

The previous story about Varda is one of my favorites. Another one (recounted with her permission) came from an artist friend. Sally quickly took to "yowling" while painting — surely an "excessive" expression of emotional feeling by conventional standards. One morning when Sally was happily working away in her attic studio, her sixteen-year-old daughter responded to the doorbell. She opened the door to find the postman leaning back, looking upward. For a moment they both listened to the horrendous howls coming from the top floor of the house. "What's that?" the postman asked anxiously. "Oh, that? That's just mother," the girl responded as she reached for the mail and closed the door.

Besides her yowling, Sally also enjoyed painting nude, going farther than some others who have done this by rolling naked on the wet Mess Paintings strewn around on the floor. Describing her experience to me, she added ruefully, *"I felt marvelous until the paint began to dry on my skin."*

I particularly like to tell stories like Sally's about letting go — about enjoying irrationality and bodily freedom — before I invite an uptight CMT group to imitate me in an exercise they might be reluctant to participate in. The behavior I initiate and ask them to follow was inspired by a scene created and performed by Naomi Newman of A Traveling Jewish Theater, in *Snake*

Talk: Messages from the Mother. She plays all three characters in the piece, one of them a poor immigrant Jewish mother who at one point asks vehemently: *"Do you know what I do when I get mad? I complain. I take plenty of time. I take a chair. I complain. A long time ago they called it lamentation. I will show you how."*

The Jewish mother then encourages the audience to join her in the vocal and bodily expressions of anguish. Her body rocks back and forth, her chest heaves, her heavy breathing is audible, and the movement of her facial muscles expresses as much as her moans and groans. At the end of several minutes of lamenting, she stands up and says, *"You see how good it feels? It clears the whole digestive tract."*

After describing the Jewish mother's monologue, I ask the group to join me, and together we act out a scene of lamentation. Participating in this experience explains, better than words can, exactly what I mean by urging people to indulge in loud vocalizing and appropriate body movements during a highly emotional painting session.

The Autogenic State and CMT

The mental state associated with letting go in CMT has similarities to and origins in Luthe's work with Autogenic Training. It helps in understanding CMT to see how Luthe invented the method through practical experience as a physician.

Wolfgang Luthe was born in 1922 and spent the first part of his life in Germany. He fought in the German army on the Russian front in World War II, where he was seriously wounded. After discharge he went on to receive his medical degree in 1947. His wartime experience gave him a lifelong concern with the problem of human aggression.

In the late 1940s, while interning at a medical clinic in Hamburg, Luthe was required to use one of the arts with his patients, and chose painting. With his characteristic precision and thoroughness, he carefully explored such questions as: How many colors, and which ones, should his patients use? What size brush? What kind of paper? How long should each painting take? How many should be done at one session? Should any interpretation be given? The answers to these questions set the stage for the subsequent development of his painting method.

After completing his training Luthe went on to a medical practice specializing in diseases of the lung. His study of Johannes Schultz's success in curing asthma with his Autogenic Training (AT) technique led Luthe to devote his life to using AT in the treatment of illness, particularly psychosomatic illness. His collaboration with Schultz and his later extensive research on his own resulted in the publication by Grune & Stratton of six volumes on AT.

Autogenic Training is widely used by medical doctors in Europe, but is little known in the U.S.A. Probably the most thoroughly researched of all self-healing methods, it dates back to the late nineteenth century, when German brain researchers observed that patients were able on their own to reach a state of auto-hypnosis which appeared to facilitate healing. Many of these patients spontaneously reported feelings of heaviness or agreeable warmth in the limbs, without having these sensations suggested to them. Schultz got the idea of inverting the procedure and found that patients were able to induce a hypnosis-like state by imagining heaviness and warmth in the limbs. Inducing this state, through the repetition of verbal formulas, had a positive influence on the patients' recovery. Schultz called this trance-like state the autogenic state.

> *"It must be emphasised that AT is not 'just another' relaxation technique. The altered state of consciousness (called the AUTOGENIC STATE) which results from the practice is akin to certain meditational states. The essence of the method is letting go of the striving-for-results and becoming the passive observer. In this state, the brain's inherent, self-regulatory mechanisms function naturally, thus allowing a rebalancing of the activities of the right and left hemispheres. This in turn boosts the workings of the immune system, promotes healing processes and can bring about greater emotional balance and release of creativity."*
> - British Autogenic Society

Influenced by his wartime experiences, Luthe eventually left Germany, emigrating in 1951 with his family to Montreal, Canada — the country he considered least likely to go to war. He continued to collaborate with Schultz, and together they produced five definitive volumes on Autogenic Training, which were published in 1969.

When in 1966 Canada established the National Health System, Luthe found he could no longer devote several hours to a single patient. The long history-taking process required for prescribing a personalized program of Autogenic Training was now spread out over several weeks. Rather than delay his patients' recovery, Luthe decided to begin treatment by teaching them how to do the painting method he had created long before in Germany, while he continued to gather data. The painting process was something they could do on their own, at home, to help themselves.

AUTOGENIC EXERCISES

Standard Autogenic Exercises	Physiological Responses
SE 1. "My arms and legs are heavy."	muscular relaxation
SE 2. "My arms and legs are warm."	increased blood flow in skin
SE 3. "My heart beat is calm and regular."	slowing of heart rate and lowering of blood pressure
SE 4. "It breathes me."	slower, deeper breathing and reduced oxygen consumption
SE 5. "My solar plexus is warm."	restoration of homeostasis in the gut and other abdominal organs
SE 6. "My forehead is cool" (and clear)	inducing a state of mental calm and a clear head

- J. B. O'Donovan, *The Application of Autogenic Training in Organic Illness*

Luthe found that his patients' use of the painting method was even more successful than he had anticipated. Some patients, after only a few weeks of painting, needed no other treatment. Luthe realized for the first time that the painting technique could be a therapy on its own.

He also ascertained that with proper training it could be taught by others, not necessarily medical doctors. Desiring to facilitate the development of qualified practitioners and prevent modification and technical errors from eroding the effectiveness of the method, he wrote a textbook in which he named his painting process The Creativity Mobilization Technique (CMT).

Luthe told me that he was assisted in the preparation of his book by twenty-two volunteers. A few of these later assisted Luthe in his research and/or developed their own studies of CMT, presenting papers with Luthe and on their own at international medical and educational conferences. While studying with Luthe in Montreal I met Lucie Duranceau, head of a college art department, and psychiatrists Steven R. Blumberger and J.L.G. de Rivera. All three contributed to the advancement of CMT, and I have continued to be in occasional contact with them over the last twenty years.

The discussion in this chapter of the theory of CMT borrows heavily from the expert and succinct paper presented in 1977 by Dr. Blumberger at the Fourth Annual Conference of the National Association for Creative Children and Adults in Toronto. I am grateful to Dr. Blumberger for granting me permission to use the information in his paper freely throughout this book.

CMT has a number of features in common with Autogenic Training. In both it is necessary to learn passive concentration. The emphasis upon repetition in Autogenic Therapy is also found in CMT, where a natural rhythmical repetition of color and form begins to occur once the desired mental state of "letting go" is present during the painting session. The role of the physician or facilitator is also similar in that it is less hierarchical than in most healing disciplines. In his painting method, Luthe's role was even less authoritarian than that of the teacher in Autogenic Training. The CMT protocol encourages self-autonomy because the patient is the final expert on his own experience.

In Autogenic Therapy the patient practices the assigned exercises at home and reports to the physician all sensations that accompanied the exercises. Similiarly, in CMT the participant follows all the instructions and performs the process at home on his own, keeping a record of and later reporting on the sensations, feelings and thoughts which came up while painting.

Luthe's development of CMT in the 1960s was heavily influenced not only by Autogenic Training, but also by his interest in Oriental approaches to art. He had ample opportunity to study Zen Buddhism as well as Japanese painting and calligraphy, because he was frequently invited to Japan to teach and lecture to the biofeedback community on Autogenic Training. The Japanese, quick to recognize the value of a method to increase creativity, have translated and published Luthe's book on CMT.

> *"Process-oriented no-thought Mess Painting may be considered as an activity that tries to get away from the dualistic and product-oriented elements such as forms, words and ideas thus providing an opportunity for the inherent natural forces to interact more freely... This is essentially an idea compatible with Zen. Both in Zen poetry (chidden) and in Zen painting (gaze; zenga) the aim is to engage in a self-evolving process that avoids studied theories of conventional rules and emphasizes the subtleties resulting from an uncensored flow of natural impulses of self-expression."*
>
> - Wolfgang Luthe,
> *The Creativity Mobilization Technique*

Why CMT Works

Understanding how CMT developed out of Autogenic Training helps us to understand why letting go has a profound healing effect. Over my years of exploring body/mind/spirit relationships, I have become convinced that the core self, the instinctual self, is both healer and life bringer. It is this essentially non-verbal self that has the opportunity to express itself through the language of color, form, and body movement in CMT.

As in Autogenic Training, once the self-regulating activities of the autonomic nervous system are allowed to prevail, the inner healer has an opportunity to do its work.

Freeing the Non-Dominant Side of the Brain. CMT is also based on the recognition of a difference between the activities of the right and left cerebral hemispheres of the brain. In right-handed people, the left, or dominant, hemisphere carries out language and arithmetic functions, while the right hemisphere specializes in spatial relations and musical functions. The left hemisphere's characteristic cognitive style is analytical and logical, while the right is holistic, serving such functions as intuition, fantasy, symbolism, and probably creativity.

To stimulate creativity, then, the first step is to overcome the inhibitory influence of the left, or dominant, hemisphere. Unfortunately our schools favor such left-hemispheric functions as logical, mathematical, and verbal skills, which helps to entrench the domination of the left-hemispheric cognitive mode.

Since Mess Painting is a non-verbal, non-analytic, and visual/spatial approach, it appears to help evoke the creativity-related functions of the non-dominant right hemisphere. It is also significant that Mess Painting is performed with large arm movements involving the arm as a whole rather than the wrist and hand. Brain research indicates that fine motor control is mainly left hemispheric, while large proximal movements seem to be controlled by the non-dominant hemisphere of the brain.

Brain research has found that creativity also depends upon communication between the left and right hemispheres of the brain through the corpus callosum. Luthe believed that CMT not only evoked creativity-related functions in the non-dominant cerebral hemisphere, but also facilitated communication between the two hemispheres.

Color. During Mess Painting, it appears that there is a shift to the right hemispheric cognitive mode, and confrontation with unconscious material at a symbolic level becomes possible. Color is the language used to evoke and express this symbolic material.

When Luthe found that the physical act of painting and the concomitant exposure of the brain to large amounts of color stimulated emotion and memory, he considered it an important discovery, for it is generally acknowledged that creativity is tied to emotion. It is access to feelings that enables creative people to be imaginative.

Children start out fully in touch with their feelings and have no difficulty knowing what colors to choose to express them in their art work. In her definitive study of children's emotional expression through painting, done at the University of Chicago in 1942, Rosa Alschuler concluded that the colors children used at day care corresponded to the joy, sadness, anxiety, fear, or anger they were experiencing.

While there is no universal agreement as to the symbolic meaning of various colors, many Mess Painters begin by having certain associations with the colors, which then change in the course of their CMT program.

Brown paint is often at first a reminder of excrement, carrying associations with toilet training, smearing of feces, frustration, and aggression, and for that reason it may be avoided. On the other hand, brown can represent the rich, fertile earth, as it did for Kathleen: *"Towards the end I was using blue and green and brown and I really felt like I was in a forest, with calming feelings about earth and water and plants."*

For one person yellow is a happy color, while another's reaction to yellow paint may be nausea and a desire to vomit, or to avoid the use of yellow altogether. And when people are experiencing black paint as negative, they may need to do an astonishing number of all-black paintings to express a complicated range of negative feelings.

When a person has let go in Mess Painting, the colors become vehicles for self-expression and assist in the readjustment of psychodynamic disturbances. For example, the repeated use of red can gradually reduce a dislike of red that may have originated from a disturbing confrontation with blood and fear of death — an automobile accident, a war incident, or a bad experience with beginning menstruation. At one time red may be an expression of rage and aggression, and at another moment it may be love and valentines.

For one CMT painter, color had the power to bring about an experience of age regression — the reliving of an episode with all its emotional, mental, and physical components. Mary Anne, an ex-nun, was painting with blue and white, and as the two colors merged, she suddenly became very cold. She found herself back at her family's farmhouse as a tiny child, painfully stuck to a block of ice she was sitting on in the bathtub as punishment for having wet her panties — her mother's cruel method of toilet training. She was whimpering and calling herself "Bad girl!" and holding back her tears. She knew if she didn't cry her mother would soon lift her off the ice and put on dry, clean clothing. It is extraordinary to me that a child subjected to such torture could hold back screams of pain.

As I was sitting at my desk, writing about Mary Anne's experience in an early draft of this chapter, I recalled how my own mother would tell me, when I was crying: *"If you want to cry I'll give you something to cry about."* Her threat of a spanking shut me up and dried my tears. Having to learn self-control far too early meant that as an adult, until I found ways of working on this problem — through Eriksonian and Gestalt therapy, CMT and Autogenic Training — I *couldn't* cry when I wanted and needed to.

My office window was open that afternoon, and from the house next door came the wails of a small child and the stern voice of a woman: *"I told you NO! You can't play with it."* The wails increased and over them I heard: *"Do you want me to give you something to REALLY cry about?"*

There it was — another mother forbidding excessive emotional expression, preparing her child to knuckle under and lose touch with her true feelings. Most likely this child will develop into an adult who will have great difficulty in being emotionally expressive, and will lack contact with her innate creativity.

Repetition. Repetition is an important part of the CMT process. It occurs in repeated movements, colors, and forms, as well as in repeated confrontation with disturbing material. This confrontation facilitates the neutralization of disturbing dynamics which interfere with creativity and healing.

The repeated use of black helped Janice Crow, an artist, to retrieve a memory she had repressed since early childhood. At a group meeting she came in with an enormous stack of totally black paintings. She reported that at earlier sessions she had avoided black as it was a frightening reminder of depression. When she finally forced herself to use it, she suddenly relived being left for a long time in a playpen at eighteen months of age, bored, needing her diaper changed, and weeping. Suddenly her eighteen-year-old father was striking her again and again and yelling at her to stop crying.

Janice, the oldest of four children, had witnessed her father hit the other children and thought he must have struck her too, but she had no memory of it until that particular day of Mess Painting. As a child she had learned how to avoid her father's wrath, and had paid for that with a chronic constriction in her throat and chest which had affected the ease, quality, and range of volume of her speech all her life.

In the Mess Painting session Janice had covered sheet after sheet of paper with black paint, rocking and sobbing as she stayed with the painful memory. Occasionally her adult mind would intrude and say, *"This is enough of black,"* but the minute she put a stroke of another color down she had to use black and cover it up — as well as covering every other inch of the paper with black.

Motor Expression. The kinesthetic element of Mess Painting also helps to explain its healing power. Mess Painting, practiced regularly and correctly, provides an opportunity to release tension through motor expression, and also through the symbolic acting out of aggressive impulses. Verbal unloading and emotional self-expression — swearing, yelling, crying — are encouraged. The expression of emotions stimulated by the technique helps to reduce tension and mobilize creativity.

According to Janet Long, an art therapist and psychotherapist[1] who has referred a number of clients to me for CMT:

> *"The kinesthetic aspect of CMT, moving the whole body while painting, appears to release long-held cellular patterns in the body. For this reason CMT is an excellent therapy for persons wishing to alleviate physical tension and symptoms. CMT goes far beyond other forms of psychotherapy in this respect, freeing energy for the client to use in desired ways....*
>
> *"Loosening tension patterns in the body has profound effects for some CMT participants. One client I referred was able to free up motion in an injured arm, while another was able to release a constricted throat and find her true voice. A third was able to feel pleasant sensations in her pelvis for the first time, which was especially vital because she was trying to become pregnant."*

Paul Freeman, a psychiatrist, described an exuberant experience with the kinesthetic aspect of CMT:

> *"Late one night when I was having a particularly wild session, happily splashing, slashing the paint onto the newspaper with my whole body involved, I began to move all around my small table as I painted . . . suddenly I threw down my brush and flung open the garage doors. I danced and twirled up and down the street feeling as though any minute I would be dancing on the sides of the apartment buildings like Gene Kelly in* An American in Paris.*"*

Soon after, Paul developed an interest in rock art, which now endlessly fascinates him and takes him to remote places all over the world.

Paradoxical Approaches. CMT achieves some of its effects through the operation of paradox. Thus, confronting dirty colors in Mess Paintings tends to stimulate a desire for cleaner, brighter colors; messiness stimulates a

> *"Children cannot tense their muscles as powerfully as grown-ups can; this makes for greater sensitivity (vulnerability) and better learning."*
>
> - Moshe Feldenkrais

desire for orderliness; and repetition can paradoxically stimulate a desire for variety and thereby enhance creativity.

Carl's music messing exercises, described earlier in this chapter, are a good example of the principle of paradoxical intention — namely, that fantasizing the very things that are feared, and acting them out in privacy within the safety of the painting process, can lead to desensitization to disturbing material. With his cardboard audience and his messy musical performances, Carl exposed himself repeatedly to the very situation that he most feared, and by doing so managed to desensitize himself to his stage fright.

All the benefits described in this chapter are dependent upon creating an environment which will facilitate letting go while you paint. This task is described in detail in the next chapter.

PROCEDURAL ELEMENTS AND STRATEGIES IN CMT ARE DESIGNED:

- *to provide environmental security for uninhibited self-expression.*

- *to eliminate interferences from environmental stimuli (radio, telephone, people, etc.)*

- *to emphasize process-oriented rather than product-oriented activity.*

- *to use visual stimuli in a self-produced feedback situation (certain colors).*

- *to allow ample opportunity for thematic repetition.*

- *to provide ample opportunity for self-confrontation.*

- *to discourage product-oriented preoccupations and perfectionistic performance habits.*

- *to eliminate elements related to the "work-success-reward" pattern.*

- *to create a developmental situation that permits improvement of intra- and interhemispheric interaction.*

(Continued)

- *to encourage easy discharge of aggressive impulses without eliciting feelings of guilt, punishment, or counter-aggression.*
- *to promote and facilitate other self-regulatory forms of discharges such as crying, gagging, vocal and other noise making.*
- *to aim at "desensitization" as well as "sensitization."*
- *to make ample use of paradoxical approaches — law of causation by the opposite.*
- *to be oneself, with oneself and for oneself.*
- *to develop receptivity to messages from within.*
- *to provide ample opportunity for "experimentation" and inventiveness without risk.*
- *to promote detachment from time and space and promote onset of situational fusion and "getting lost in the present."*
- *to facilitate the expression of emotional reactions.*
- *to neutralize anticreative attitudes.*

- Selected from Wolfgang Luthe's list in
Creativity Mobilization Technique

---

[1]Janet Long is a licensed Marriage, Child, and Family Counselor and a Board Certified Art Therapist, who combines her private practice with teaching medical art therapy at the University of California at Berkeley.

Chapter Three

Preparation

*"The only way to learn something
is to do it. There is no other way."*

- John Holt, Educator

Although CMT provides extraordinary pleasures, they probably will not be present while you are getting set up. Indeed, there may be moments when you will regret having committed yourself to this adventure. Let me assure you that Mess Painting will not only yield a variety of healing benefits, but it will also provide you with hours of joyful, creative fun.

As one Mess Painter described it:

"That first week was absolute hell. I wanted to paint, not cope with finding a work space. I hated buying supplies — that's just like what I do all the time, and don't want to be doing ever. And then came the maddening job of putting up plastic to protect the walls and ceiling. I complained to my husband every day. He asked reasonably why I was torturing myself. That doubled my anger because all I could think to say was 'because I want to!' I finally finished the setup, and the pain involved in birthing my very own place to mess with paint was forgotten in the excitement of covering the paper with the wonderful, sensuous colors."

Perhaps the words of Sir George Wade will inspire you and keep you going as difficulties arise. An eighty-seven-year-old retired ceramics manufacturer, Wade was living in rural England in 1977 when he wrote these observations on painting. He died in 1985. I was given permission to quote from his unpublished essay by his daughter Iris, the Englishwoman who appears in my documentary film (see Chapter 2).

Sir George painted landscapes and portraits most of his adult life until, in his later years, he discovered the joy of abstract painting — a type of art he had always scoffed at as the refuge of the incompetent artist, the happy hunting ground of charlatans who prey upon gullible people. He arrived at an entirely different view when he was given a little book on abstract painting:

"Its message was simply this. When you decide to do an abstract painting you should have no idea what you aspire to paint and while you are painting you should have no thoughts about what you are creating. Thus and only thus can you produce a genuine abstract work of art.

"I started working on the lines suggested, and before I had produced many abstract paintings as laid down in this formula, the GREAT TRUTH began to dawn on me. It is just this: an ordinary, honest to God, straight forward, photographic type of painting is produced by a great concentrated effort of your conscious mind, whereas a genuine abstract is a creation of your subconscious mind, two vastly differing experiences.

"After that, it was easy. I found great joy in letting myself go with paint ... free and unhindered ... no attention on drawing, composition, texture, color or harmony. I just handed myself happily to my subconscious mind.

"After a couple of hours spent this way in a sort of delicious trance, I would emerge with my mind eased of the tensions of having to share the Earth with so many odd people and feel relaxed as if I had just had a week's vacation.

"These spontaneous paintings have a wonderful and lasting charm for me which grows and grows. If I paint something in the old-fashioned photographic style, I may feel quite pleased with it and hang it on my bedroom wall, but in a week or two I never even see it as I pass by. Not so with an abstract! Every time I look at it I see unexpected and hitherto unseen beauty. It is like a series of pegs on which my imagination can hook itself and see strange, satisfying and wonderful

things. When I get out of bed on a cold winter morning, it catches my eye and I stand gazing at it before I even put on my robe. No need for drugs or booze if you can lose yourself in abstract painting."

"Of course, it's a messy hobby but we are all entitled to a small corner of our very own on this earth, before we are actually in it. SO! Go to it, my friends! Get yourselves a flat working surface, some paints, brushes — a small corner which is YOURS and YOURS alone."

Sir George's enthusiasm for abstract painting could apply equally well to the rewards of Mess Painting. In fact his daughter bemoaned the fact that I couldn't be cloned and give CMT in England at the same time I was doing it in California.

But before the rewards comes the challenging task of creating the physical and psychological environment that will facilitate having a unique adventure with Mess Painting.

Time Commitment

It is very important to choose an appropriate two-month period. That means checking your appointment calendar to find a time when you haven't scheduled a number of long weekends, or a vacation of a week or more, away from home. Ideally you should not have more than one or two long weekend jaunts planned during the seven weeks of your CMT program. If you must leave home for a whole week, try to organize your painting schedule so that your one week away will fall either between the first and second weeks of CMT, or after six consecutive weeks of painting.

CMT produces the best results if you consistently paint on four different days each week for at least seven consecutive weeks. If you must interrupt that ideal schedule then plan to paint two weeks longer, or more. You may find you want to do that anyway.

Each painting session (including the necessary record keeping and time for reflection) will take one and one-half to two hours. In order to make room in your life for the required amount of painting, you may need to make adjustments in your lifestyle. You may decide to "create" more time in your day by getting up an hour earlier, or staying up later at night. Please postpone signing up for other classes during your CMT program. No matter how eager you are to start CMT, if you are presently enrolled in a demanding class please wait until it has ended before you begin your painting program.

Cost of Materials

You are probably wondering how much your CMT program will cost. I tell people it will cost approximately $165 for materials. That figure allows for eight gallons of paint at $10.95 each, but many people find they need more. Many tempera paints cost more, and shipping costs will vary with your location. Once you get into the swing of Mess Painting, you will understand the importance of being willing to spend what is necessary to ensure an adequate supply of paint. Among beginning Mess Painters, resistance to the expense of large quantities of paint is a commonly noted impediment to letting go.

Work Space

Setting up a pleasant, efficient place for CMT — one that reduces opportunities for self-sabotage — may be fun and easy for you, or it may present numerous challenges. If you are not experienced with art materials, you may find the setup process frustrating; or you may enjoy the opportunity to become familiar with simple, inexpensive paints, brushes, and paper, as did writer Ann Keiffer:

"In these years of my middle-aging, I am discovering a deep need to be in touch with my body's experience, needs, and wisdom. Perhaps because of this heightened awareness, in the months before I turned fifty-one, I began to notice fleeting sensations of wet paint on my hands and feet, as if my hands and feet were moving slowly and sensually across a surface covered with wet paint. Not being a complete dolt, I thought perhaps I needed to paint! But on the two occasions I

went to the art supply store, I just stood in the aisles becoming more and more confused and art-shy. What was the right kind of paper? What was the right kind of paint? What was the right kind of brush? I was so bewildered and cowed by the mystique of being an artist, I had to leave the store without buying a single thing. I just did not see myself as a person with artistic talent or any sense of how to begin, so how could I ever hope to paint?

"But the sensation of wet paint stayed with me. When I heard about Mess Painting, I knew immediately it was exactly the kind of structure I needed in order to begin painting — nothing precious or high-falutin' about it, plain old newspaper, elementary school paints, and kiddie brushes."

The instructions that follow are highly detailed in order to help those who have never done anything like this before. If you are not yet certain that you are going to undertake CMT, you may want to skip the rest of this chapter for now, and go on to Chapter 4.

The first requirement is to find an area where the setup can remain for the duration of your painting program; otherwise four times a week you will be arranging, removing, storing, and rearranging the things you use while painting. The extra time and work an impermanent setup requires could be very frustrating.

I have seen exceptions to this general caveat, however. Marge, a seventy-year-old woman, was adamant that she had no place to paint except in her tiny kitchen. She insisted that since she lived alone and her time was not committed to doing anything else, it would not be a problem to move everything in and out of the kitchen for each painting session. Marge was so determined to experience CMT fully that she followed through and completed her sessions on schedule, under conditions that might have caused others to give up.

Generally Mess Painters choose to work in a corner of their garage, laundry room, or basement, or in a part of their dining room, living room, bedroom, or enclosed porch. People often ask about painting out of doors, but very few have managed to do so because wind, rain, and temperature changes usually present insurmountable problems. However, if you live in a mild, dry climate and have a space that is private, without wind, where cats or dogs will not disturb your paintings as they are drying, where you can string up some lights and paint at night as well as during the day, and where neighbors cannot see or hear you, then painting out of doors can be a joy.

One advantage to having your work area in your home is that you can paint in the middle of the night when a problem is keeping you awake. If your living situation is such that you cannot create the space you need at home, and if none of your friends have a corner you could use, try contacting churches and recreation centers, and look on bulletin boards in art stores for ads placed by artists wanting to share their studios. One Mess Painter was able to rent space in the basement of a church for a very reasonable fee.

In choosing your painting area, consider whether there will be sufficient air circulation, and whether you can regulate the temperature so that you are not too hot or too cold. Take dampness into consideration, since the paintings must dry in time to make room for the next batch. The careful use of an electric heater or fan will help to maintain your physical comfort and expedite drying the paintings.

It is best to paint in a space where you will feel free to make some noise. You may be reluctant to sing or yell if you think your neighbors can hear you. One way to find out is to place a radio on your work table, turn up the volume and then ask your neighbors if they can hear it. Perhaps they will allow you to come in and out to experiment with raising and lowering the volume to see at what point it is audible in their living space.

If you discover that your walls are not soundproofed sufficiently and if your neighbors are home most of the time, you may need to postpone noise-making and do it elsewhere. A radio cannot be used to camouflage sound, since talk shows or lectures would be distracting, and music could change your mood or influence your thoughts. While Mess Painting, you are to allow thoughts and emotions to come and go on their own, without any influence other than the colors of the paint and the brush work. The only sounds in your work space are to be those of your own making.

As Karen discovered, being able to make noise is part of the larger benefit of having a truly private space of one's own:

"It felt like quite a big risk to me to babble and screech and howl and groan and laugh and cry, but it also felt like a real gift to myself. Which brings me to another awareness that came after I began vocalizing more, which was that in some ways, though not all, the painting is just a device — a tool, an excuse, or something like that — to lure us into a physical space, a time space, an emotionally safe and free place that is all our own, to do with entirely as we please. That also felt like a real gift to me. It's incredible that we, or at least I, don't get up off my ass and create that kind of space for myself on my own, but it seems out of inertia or hopelessness or something many of us don't."

I do want to emphasize that if you have no alternative but to paint in a noise-restricted environment you will get good results nonetheless. Success with CMT is not solely dependent upon free vocal expression. Over the years quite a few of my clients have had to paint in noise-restricted places. Despite the lack of freedom for vocal exploration while painting, most of them were very pleased with their CMT experience.

Floor Plan

The drawing at the top of the next page (page 74) shows one possible floor plan. Whether you can store the gallons of paint where they are readily accessible, or whether you must store them under your work table, depends upon how much room you have. The numbered newspapers may be hung over the back of a chair, or kept on the table if it is large enough. You need a piece of carpet on which to stand, and a stack of 24 drying trays. The trays can be stored against the wall until they are used. Please take your time in arranging these objects. It will be very helpful to your success if you can move from one painting to the next with the greatest economy of motion.

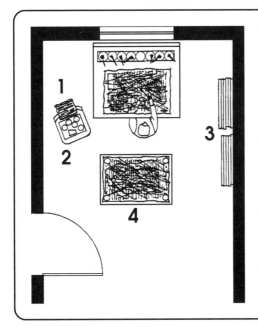

FLOOR PLAN

1. Newspapers are hanging over the back of the chair.

2. Box of risers is on the seat of the chair.

3. Drying trays waiting to be used are leaning against the wall.

4. Completed paintings are stacked on trays with risers.

Protecting Walls, Ceiling, and Floor

Whatever area you use — living quarters or garage, covered porch or a shed in the garden — you will need to protect the walls, ceiling, and floor from flying paint. House painters' drop cloths of clear plastic can be used for this purpose — very thin for the ceiling and heavier for the walls. To protect the floor, you may prefer a paper drop cloth backed with plastic rather than plain, heavy plastic. If you use plastic, you can lay large corrugated cardboard sheets or flattened boxes on top to make it safer to walk on the slippery surface.

If your walls or ceiling do not permit the use of staples, the plastic drop cloths can be attached with many small pieces of masking tape or two-sided tape. Art supply stores sell a double-sided tape that is used for exhibitions and will not mar painted surfaces.

Make a test on an area normally out of view (behind a picture, a piece of furniture or a lighting fixture) if you want to be sure the tape will not leave a mark.

Jill, a young businesswoman, demonstrated that even the most elegant of environments can be protected. Her living room had two-inch thick, pale blue carpeting and fine teak-paneled walls. Jill created her painting area by moving furniture out of one corner of the room and putting plastic over part of two walls and part of the ceiling. To separate her painting area from the rest of the room, she created a third wall by using flexible one-inch by three-inch wooden battens (available at lumber yards), about one inch longer than the height of the ceiling, to keep the plastic in place. The two plastic-covered room walls and one temporary wall of plastic and battens created a rectangular space eight feet long — long enough so that Jill did not have to hang a protective plastic curtain across the fourth, or open, side. A plastic-backed paper drop cloth was placed over the carpet inside and beyond her painting area, and for additional comfort and safety, carpet samples were laid down both inside and outside the area. When Jill finished a painting session, she was careful to step out of her paint-spattered coveralls and old shoes before walking on her protective runway to the kitchen where she would drink a cup of tea while relaxing and writing in her Journal.

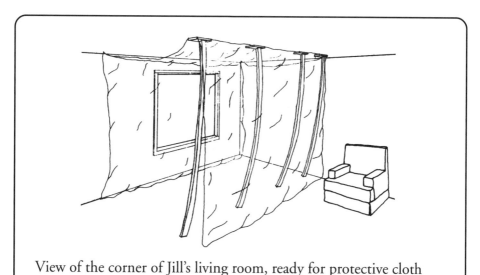

View of the corner of Jill's living room, ready for protective cloth on the floor, work table, and painting supplies.

Lighting

Good, bright light over your working area is important so that the colors of the paint will have their full impact on you. One ceiling fixture is never sufficient — unless it happens to be a four-foot fluorescent hanging directly above where you will be painting. Bare bulbs at the end of extension cords hung from a hook in the ceiling will do as well as fancy lamps. You will need at least 300 watts of light.

Because incandescent and most fluorescent bulbs cast a yellowish light and alter the appearance of the paint, a full-spectrum 150-watt light, the kind used for growing plants indoors, is very helpful as part of your illumination. These are available at hardware stores or nurseries; a 150-watt light costs under $10.00. Be sure to arrange the light source over your working surface so that you are not painting in your own shadow, and <u>avoid hanging a fluorescent fixture too low over your working surface</u>, or the light will give the wet paint an unpleasant shine. Even if your table is next to a window and you find you prefer to paint during the day, it is still advisable to create a setup that permits an occasional night session.

"Do Not Disturb" Sign

A "DO NOT DISTURB" sign on the door to your painting space will help ensure your privacy. Put it up even when your housemates are gone, as they might return unexpectedly.

Checklists

When you shop for your supplies, be sure to bring this book along and make at least seven photocopies of the Checklist in Chapter 5. You will need one Checklist for each week you do CMT.

Table and Work Surface

The material recommended for your work surface is fiberboard. Fiberboard is also called "sound stop." It is not the same as particle board, which is smooth, lighter in color, very heavy, and much more expensive. It is not OSB board. When fiberboard first came on the market, it was called Cellutex. It often comes with one side painted white; you should use the unpainted surface. Fiberboard is sold at lumber yards in sheets four by eight feet. For a small charge the lumber yard will cut it for you. Fiberboard is fairly soft and, if you need or want to, you can cut it yourself with a sharp-edged utility knife. The size of your table or other base, and the size of the car used for transporting it home, determine the measurements for the cuts to be made at the lumber yard. The minimum size for a working surface is 36" by 42". It is desirable to have two thicknesses, since a single thickness tends to warp or bend. Your car may be too small to accommodate pieces cut to the minimum dimensions of 36" by 42". If so, you may need to borrow a larger vehicle, or plan the cuts so that you can glue the top and bottom pieces together.

Another possibility for the working surface is plywood. Since fiberboard

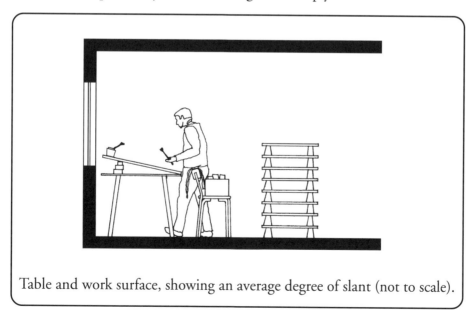

Table and work surface, showing an average degree of slant (not to scale).

is much less expensive, use plywood only if you already have some of a suitable size. Plywood needs to be tightly covered with thin plastic that is stapled or taped underneath; otherwise its rough surface will tear your wet paintings. The drawing on page 77 shows a fiberboard or plywood work surface, propped up to create the desired degree of slant. The eight paint-filled containers are sitting at the back of the work surface in a wallpapering trough (described below).

Until recently I thought fiberboard and plywood were the only choices for a working surface, but some people have found other solutions. Grant bought a four-foot section of a used Formica kitchen counter top and adapted it to his needs with scrap wood. Kathryn, who had recently remodeled her house, had an old window with a metal sash. The measurement of the window-pane was larger than the dimensions suggested for the fiberboard, and she liked the fact that the metal frame caught the excess water and paint she slopped on the glass. The window couldn't warp, and it was easy to install on a slant, on top of a table of appropriate height, by placing pieces of scrap two-by-fours under the back edge of the metal sash. However, when Sherry borrowed Kathryn's window she found that the metal frame felt confining, and chose to use fiberboard instead.

The degree of slant is a matter of personal preference and is related to body size. A slanted work surface is essential for a petite person with short arms, and is usually desirable for a taller person as well. When creating the slant, be sure that the working surface remains firm and does not wobble or bend in the middle.

No matter what kind of base you use, you need to check the height of the working surface and adjust it, if necessary, so that you do not experience any back strain. If you are plagued with back problems, it is especially important that both the height and the slant of the working surface are fine-tuned for your comfort. If the working surface is too low, place scrap wood, books or bricks under the legs of your table, or use them on top of the table to build up the height of the working surface. Wheelchair-bound Mess Painters need to take special care to adjust the height and slant of their work surface.

Paper

Newspaper rather than plain paper is used in Mess Painting because there is a natural resistance to making the biggest possible mess on a pristine sheet of white paper. Paper that will absorb paint and is the size of a newspaper is very expensive. Butcher paper is too glossy, and plain newsprint would be hard to find large enough. In any case both are poor choices because their plain, unmarked surfaces tend to create barriers to messy painting. Old newspaper on its way to recycling is the best choice.

However, not just any newspaper will do: it must be *The Wall Street Journal,* or a paper of equal or larger dimensions. *The Wall Street Journal* is larger than most other newspapers, measuring approximately 22 by 29 inches. Its 29-inch width encourages a longer brush stroke. Some people have discovered other appropriately sized newspapers. Michelle, who flew up every week from Los Angeles for a CMT group, found a Korean paper wider and longer than *The Wall Street Journal.* She enjoyed the appearance of the Oriental typeface, and since it was printed in Korean she wasn't tempted to read it. Another painter, Maggie, found an agricultural newspaper which was larger and heavier in weight than *The Wall Street Journal.*

People usually look astonished when I insist they use <u>*The Wall Street Journal.*</u> One client wrote: *"When you told us we had to use <u>The Wall Street Journal</u> I said to myself, 'Oh, come on, lady; that's ridiculous' — but the day I ran out of the Journal and had to use the <u>Chronicle</u> I found out why. It seemed unpleasantly small and I didn't like its squarer shape."*

You can find sources for *The Wall Street Journal* by putting flyers on bulletin boards. Some people pretend they will be using the paper for a children's art project to avoid having to explain Mess Painting. Your neighbor, library, bank, doctor, lawyer, broker, or insurance agent may subscribe. Two or three subscribers could furnish you with more than you require. Or perhaps you can find a distributor of the paper who is willing to give you excess copies.

Well before you begin your first painting session, gather a pile of *Wall*

Street Journals. Open them out, issue by issue and page by page, to create a stack of full-spread sheets. *Remove all half sheets.* Organize the newspapers so the print on each sheet is lined up as it would be for reading and begin to number them. With a broad-tip waterproof marking pen, place the numbers in the lower right-hand corner about three inches in from the edge of the paper. Make them large — two or three inches high. Start with number 1 and continue until you have at least 150 numbered. The next stack you number will start with 151. If you have collected enough papers, there is no reason except fatigue not to number right away up to five hundred — the minimum number of full-spread sheets you will need for seven weeks of painting.

Numbering a great many newspapers at one time allows complete freedom in the number of paintings you will do at any one session. If you wait and number newspapers just before beginning to paint, you may predetermine how many paintings you will create. It would be an error to number only twenty-four, even though that is four more than the maximum of twenty suggested for one session, because on occasion you may need to paint more than that and you are less likely to do so if you run out of numbered newspapers.

Paint

Eight gallons of water-based school tempera paint are needed to start with — one each of black, white, brown, red, yellow, blue, green and violet (purple).

Not every brand of paint is suitable, since the right colors are necessary in CMT to produce the desired effects on eye and brain as you work with them. The brown should be a rich, warm, reddish brown, not the color of dark chocolate or milk chocolate. The green should not be a Christmasy shade, but rather a brighter and lighter green that suggests vegetation. The violet should be an intense, rich purple, not a dull lavender. Red will not have the same effect if it is even slightly fluorescent, or a bit on the orange side. The yellow in some brands is too pale and too transparent; you want a nice, bright yellow, not one that has a gold or greenish cast. Blue must be a true, strong, bright ultramarine blue. You do not want a dark dull blue, nor one that has a slightly greenish hue. Inadequate blue is by far the most common paint selection problem. Although there are color reproductions of Mess Paintings in this book, it is impossible for a printer to reproduce the original colors exactly. They are probably 95 percent like the originals.

Retail art supply stores generally carry tempera paint only in pint sizes, but many brands can be ordered by the gallon. School supply stores are a good source of gallon sizes. If you do not live near an art or school supply store, or are too busy to shop, or if the colors of the paint your store carries do not come close to matching those specified, you can have paint shipped directly to your home via UPS. The name and address of a large mail order school art supply company, and the brand of paint I recommend, is listed below.

PAINT AND BRUSHES

1. **PAINT:** Water-based school tempera paints. TempraTone brand is recommended. You will need one gallon each of black, white, brown, red, yellow, blue, green, violet (purple).

2. **BRUSHES:** Natural-bristle brush, 3/4" wide. I recommend "So Big," manufactured by the Crayola Company. You will need 8 brushes, one for each color, plus 3 or 4 extra. They are cheaper by the dozen.

Paint and brushes are available from Morrison School Supplies, 400 Industrial Blvd, San Carlos, CA 94070, phone: 1-800-950-4567. They can ship your order via UPS.

A gallon of each color may not be enough for your twenty-eight (or more) sessions. Some people apply more paint than others, or use a larger amount of some colors. *Do not sabotage your experience by scrimping on paint.* If some of your colors are being used up faster than others, *buy more before you run out.*

For your painting sessions, you will need to decant the paint from the eight gallon bottles into eight one-pint containers (See page 83, "Trough"). The paint containers should be made of plastic, not glass or metal, as paint will build up permanently on the edges of glass or metal.

As you open the gallons of paint and begin decanting them into the smaller containers, you may discover that the paint varies in consistency. One color may be thin and another very thick. Pouring out the paint may be easy in one case and difficult in others.

At the first CMT group meeting I always mention this problem, and offer the obvious solution: *"When the paint is thick, add some water. Keep testing to see that the brush can move easily over the paper. Be careful not to add too much water, because the paint must not be so thin that it is transparent."* It amazes me that some people find this direction frustrating. How can the simple job of altering the consistency of one or two of the colors become an issue of major proportions and a source of great distress? But it sometimes has. Over your first few painting sessions, through trial and error, you will arrive at the right consistency. As a rule of thumb, the paint is probably too thin if you can easily read the newspaper through it; if it is too thick it will take effort to move the brush and the paint will crack as it dries, and will later fall off the paper.

Some people don't like the smell of tempera paint, especially as it tends to ferment when left standing. Try burning incense, or adding salt to the paint, or a few drops of pine oil disinfectant (available at grocery stores), or oil of eucalyptus or wintergreen (from drugstores or health food stores).

Trough

After the paint has been brought to the right consistency in the pint containers, the containers are placed in a plastic wallpapering trough. These are very inexpensive, and are available wherever wallpaper is sold. Using a trough has several advantages. First, it simplifies covering the paints between sessions so they won't dry out. Lids won't fit once there is paint on the edges, and stretching a length of ordinary kitchen plastic wrap over the whole trough is easier than covering each container individually. Having the paint containers in a trough will prevent them from being knocked off the working surface. Also, you can place a narrow length of wood under the trough toward the back edge, so that it slants down toward you. This makes it easier to move the brushes in and out of the paint.

Some plastic pint containers measure three and five-eighths inches across the top, while others are four inches wide. If yours measure four inches you will need to buy two troughs. Cut one end off each trough and discard it. Overlap the cut ends of the trough so that there will be just enough room for your eight four-inch-diameter plastic cups to fit inside. Fasten the overlapped edges, inside and out, with gray duct tape or heavy plastic tape. If your pint-size containers are the taller, narrower shape, you will need only one trough. After you have placed these cups snugly next to each other in the trough, there will be some room left at one end. Put rags or whatever in this space; if the eight cups are spaced apart, they will be wobbly and the paint may spill. Now fill the containers until they are three-quarters full.

Brushes

The best inexpensive natural-bristle brush I have found is one designed for children called "So Big," manufactured by the Crayola Company. This brush has a round tapered handle six and one-quarter inches long. The bristles are three-quarters of an inch wide, and extend one and one-half inch beyond the handle. Retail art stores generally do not sell them; you can order these by phone or mail; they are cheaper by the dozen (See page 81).

You need one brush for each color, plus three or four extras for those times when a brush is dropped into dust on the floor or into the wrong paint container. With extra brushes available you can just throw the contaminated brush into a bucket of water, grab another and continue painting.

Timepiece

During the first week, it is important to develop a sense of timing. You need to be able to judge when two minutes have elapsed, because when you are Mess Painting you are not to spend more than two minutes on any one painting. The longer you Mess Paint on a particular painting, the more likely you are to become actively involved in making aesthetic choices. On the other hand, you need to paint long enough on each piece of newspaper to experience the impact of the colors you are using. Through clinical trials, Luthe determined that in a short period of time, closer to two minutes than one minute, most people could cover ninety percent of a newspaper measuring 22 by 29 inches using three-quarter-inch-wide natural bristle brushes, and that this amount of time permitted the brain to respond to the colors being used.

Automatic timers cannot be used for this time-sense training, because the ticking sound and bell are disturbing and can interfere with achieving an effortless flow from one painting to the next. A large clock or watch with a visible second hand, placed where you can easily see it, will work quite well. You can use an hourglass-type egg timer by putting small pieces of masking tape on the glass to mark the height of the sand at two minutes.

Drying the Paintings

The most practical way to dry your wet paintings is on drying trays that you stack one above the other as the session proceeds. Plastic or paper cups (called risers) are placed at the four corners of each drying tray in order to support the next tray. When the stack is about twelve trays high, it is advisable to start building up another stack. Higher stacks are difficult to reach and have a tendency to sag, wobble, and fall over.

You need at least twenty-four drying trays. However, this number allows for only a few more than the average output of fifteen to twenty paintings per session, and while four extra trays may be sufficient for most sessions, they may fall short of what is needed for a very emotional session. Many of my CMT clients have found twenty-four trays to be too few and have provided themselves with at least six more. Approximately ten percent have needed more than thirty trays. In any case, have a plan in mind for where you can put extra paintings to dry if you run out of trays in one of your sessions.

Even if you have a large work space where you could spread a whole session of paintings out on the floor, it is preferable to stack them, for a number of reasons. First, stacking will make it easier to keep them in the right numerical sequence. Reviewing your paintings in the correct sequence — the order in which they were painted — is absolutely necessary for making useful evaluations. Second, stacking assists the ease and speed with which you go to the next painting after putting one to dry. It takes less time to build up and undo the stacks than it does to put paintings down on the floor and pick them up after they are dried. Finally, if the paintings are spread out on the floor, each time you put another one to dry you will be able to see all you have done so far. That is not desirable, because you might stop to look at them, which is both time consuming and an interruption; and seeing what you have done on several paintings may influence what you do on the next.

The drying trays are made either of half-inch or three-quarter-inch polystyrene "bead board," or of two thicknesses of corrugated cardboard which have been glued together and covered with a plastic garden trash bag. The trays need to be two feet by three feet in size.

Polystyrene Drying Trays. Polystyrene shelving, or "bead board," is easy to cut with a utility knife with either removable or snap-off blades. Both varieties of knives, and extra blades, are sold at hardware stores. While polystyrene is easy to cut, it creates a certain amount of sawdust-like debris. If you can avoid cutting it at home, so much the better. It is also fragile, and if you carry large pieces from the store, the slightest breeze may cause them to break. It is advisable either to buy it already cut to a size you can carry safely to your car, or to cut it yourself in the store.

Large discount stores such as Home Depot carry polystyrene two-by-four-foot sheets in two thicknesses, half-inch and three-quarter-inch. The three-quarter-inch thickness is preferred. You will probably be able to get this size into your car, and once home you can cut one foot off each piece. (Save the extra one-foot pieces and fasten three together by gluing cardboard strips under the cracks, creating a "bonus" tray for every three you have made.)

You can also buy polystyrene, or bead board, at stores that sell a variety of plastic products such as acrylic sheets and fiberglass. These stores, in my experience, only carry sheets that are eight feet long, two feet wide and one-half inch thick. While they won't cut them down for their customers, I have been able to find enough space in the display room to cut them myself using a utility knife, straight edge, marking pen, and ruler or tape measure that I have brought with me. Had I not been able to do this, I would have insisted that they wrap the sheets I was buying in heavy paper so I could get them home safely in a borrowed van.

Cardboard Drying Trays. Corrugated cardboard, which can be bought in art supply stores, is also a good choice for making drying trays. This material has the advantage of being sturdier. The polystyrene trays are lighter and easier to store and move around, but without careful handling they will not last as long. The cardboard trays are more expensive, and take more time to prepare. In addition to cutting them down from larger sheets, you need to glue two two-by-three-foot pieces together before wrapping them tightly in a plastic garden trash bag. If single sheets are used, they will warp severely from the weight of the wet paintings and become unusable.

Corrugated cardboard comes in sheets six feet by three feet. Two sheets of cardboard will make three drying trays two by three feet. Therefore, you need to buy at least sixteen sheets, and I suggest you buy eighteen. Usually the art supply store will be willing to cut them for you for a fee. Some stores have a wall-mounted cutter available to customers. Cardboard can also be cut with an electric Skil saw or table saw.

If your car is not large enough to transport uncut cardboard sheets and the store does not have a cutter or space available for you to use, you may be able to do the cutting in the parking lot. Along with the necessary yardstick, marking pen, and utility knife, bring some extra blades to replace those that become dull from contact with concrete.

Use white (Elmer's) or carpenter's glue to glue two pieces of cardboard together. The glue need not be spread evenly from edge to edge; just place glue near the edges and some in the center. Then stack the double sheets of cardboard and put some heavy weights on top to keep them flat. Later when the glue has dried, slip each double piece of cardboard into a garden trash

---

BUILDING YOUR DRYING TRAYS

Dimensions of drying trays: 2′ x 3′   Number of trays needed: 24-30

1. Polystyrene Shelving ("Bead Board")
   - Available from home supply stores in 2′ x 4′ sheets, in 1/2″ and 3/4″ thickness; 3/4″ is recommended. Cut 1′ off each sheet. (Save the extra pieces and glue three 1′ pieces together with cardboard strips under the two cracks to make another tray.)
   - Available from plastic products stores in 8′ x 2′ sheets, 1/2″ thick. Cut each sheet into 2 pieces 3′ x 2′; use the leftover pieces to make extra trays as above.

2. Corrugated Cardboard
   - Available at art supply stores in 6′ x 3′ sheets.
   - Cut each sheet into three 2′ x 3′ pieces.
   - Glue two 2′ x 3′ pieces together to make a double thickness, using white or carpenter's glue. Stack the double sheets and weight them until dry.
   - Slip each double piece of cardboard into a large garden trash bag (make sure the bag is large enough to accommodate the 2′ x 3′ cardboard). Tape to fit and fasten open end with plastic packaging tape.

bag. Check the dimensions of the bags you buy to make sure they will hold the two-by-three-foot cardboard. If the bags are too wide, fold over the excess and fasten it down securely with two-inch-wide plastic packaging tape. Also fasten the bag at the open end with the tape.

Risers. Cups are used as risers to form spaces between the drying trays, keeping the trays and their paintings separated from each other. The risers must not be too tall or the stack of drying trays will become very wobbly. On the other hand, unless you have a warm, well-ventilated work area, very short risers will not allow enough air to circulate over the paintings and they will take longer to dry. Supermarkets sell plastic-coated paper cups, clear plastic party glasses, and styrofoam cups that range between two and three inches high. Whatever you use, they should be within these measurements.

Drying with Fan, Heater, or Heat Lamps. Drying your paintings is an important consideration. If you discover that they are not drying in time for you to empty the trays for the next painting session, you will need to create better air circulation by opening a window, using a fan, or placing a heater in the room (be careful to keep it away from flammable materials).

There is another way to solve the problem of drying the paintings, but it almost requires the skills of a licensed electrician. One of my clients, Alfred, reasoned rightly that several 250-watt infrared heat lamps shining down on a painting would dry it quickly. Alfred built a stand and found he needed five lamps to do the job in the time available before the next painting was completed and needed to go under the lights. [WARNING: The total wattage is close to that of a hot plate or an electric heater and could be enough to blow a fuse or trigger a circuit breaker, so do not attempt this solution unless you are experienced in working with electricity.]

As Alfred moved each dry painting from under the lights, he placed it face down on top of the previous one. When he finished a painting session, all of his work was dry and in numerical order, ready to be reviewed at the end of the week.

Storing the Paintings

When the paintings are dry, keeping them flat — not rolled or folded — will make them easy to handle when you are reviewing them. Before storing them, you need to clip together the paintings from each session with clothespins, giant paper clips, or large spring clips. You also need to separate each week's work from the next with a piece of paper appropriately labeled.

Some people store their paintings under a bed. Paul Freeman, the psychiatrist who became an avid collector of rock art, continues to keep his stack of Mess Paintings on the floor of a little closet under some stairs. He uses them to wrap the reproductions of cave art and pictographs he gives to friends, and expects never to buy gift wrapping paper again.

Miscellaneous

There are a few other items not mentioned so far. One is a loose-leaf notebook that can be used for journal writing and dream recording, or if you prefer, two separate notebooks, one for each purpose. Since you will be standing while you paint (to facilitate dance movements, large arm movements, and so forth), have a chair or stool to sit on while you write your notes about what happened.

You will need old clothes (including shoes) that are ready to be recycled, rags or a sponge to wipe up any spills, and facial tissue or paper towels in case you cry. You will also need a sponge and a bucket of water and perhaps a spray bottle to wet down your work surface. A sports bottle or glass of drinking water is optional, depending on your liquid consumption habits.

Mat and Backing

The last piece of equipment necessary for your work with CMT is a mat with a backing, for framing selected paintings. The mat is made of ordinary white mat board or pebble board. Acid-free mat board is twice as expensive and pointless to use, as your newspaper paintings are full of acid. The backing can be either two thicknesses of corrugated cardboard or 3/16-inch foam core board. Both can be purchased at the art store where you buy your mat board.

For the mat, the outside dimensions are 34 by 27 inches. You will need to cut an opening in the center (known as the "window"). The dimensions for the inner cutout are 28 by 21 inches — that is, three inches in from each edge. Some artists prefer to add an additional half inch to the bottom edge of the mat.

If you choose to use corrugated cardboard for your backing (the piece that goes underneath the mat), it should be cut *very* slightly smaller than the outside dimension of the mat. Cut two pieces — 33 $\frac{7}{8}$ by 27 $\frac{7}{8}$ inches — and glue them together with white or carpenter's glue. Have the glued pieces weighted down with books as they are drying so they won't warp. This material will be more rigid than foam core board and also cheaper, but much harder to cut neatly. If you choose to use foam core board, because it is white it can be cut to the same outside dimensions as the mat.

You will need to fasten two picture hangers to the back of the backing, and stretch a string or wire between them in order to hang the matted painting on a wall at eye level. Or get one heavy-duty foam core hanger, and reinforce it with masking tape. Any art supply store can advise you on what kind of hangers to buy and how to attach them.

Whether you cut the mat (the top piece with the window) or have it cut, you will need linen tape or duct tape to hinge the top of the mat to the top of the backing. Place the mat right side down on a table or the floor and cut three pieces of tape. Space them out along the top edge of the mat. As you adhere one half of the piece of tape to the mat, the other half is folded back sticky side up, with the fold exactly at the top edge of the mat. Line up the backing with the mat, starting at the top edge. The backing then descends onto the mat and engages the sticky side of the tape. *Voila!* Your mat and backing are hinged.

After you hinge the mat to the backing with tape, lift up the mat and center a Mess Painting on the backing. To temporarily adhere the painting to the backing, use masking tape. Don't use a tape that will stick permanently, as you will be exchanging one painting for another every two or three days. Fold the tape so that it is double-sided and put it under the top corners of the painting. Next draw a line around the painting on the backing, to guide the placement of the next painting.

You will now need small pieces of Velcro, the kind that already has sticky glue on the back. Any color will do. You can buy Velcro at hardware or yardage stores; five inches will be more than enough for one mat.

Velcro generally comes in two strips on a piece of paper, side by side. Before removing the protective paper from the Velcro, fold the piece of paper the strips are on so that the bottom and top pieces of Velcro stick together. Then cut the five inches of stuck-together Velcro into small pieces about three-quarters inch in length (there will be some left over). Remove the protective coating from only one side of each piece. Place three pieces, glue side down, approximately halfway between the bottom edge of the painting and the bot-

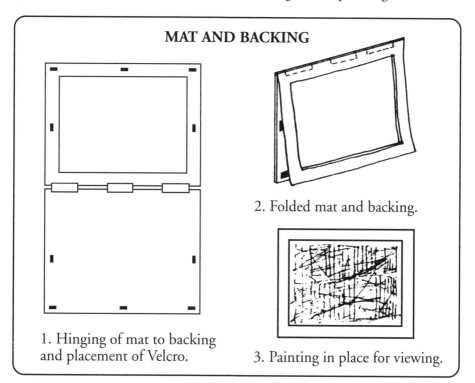

MAT AND BACKING

1. Hinging of mat to backing and placement of Velcro.

2. Folded mat and backing.

3. Painting in place for viewing.

tom edge of the backing, and one piece on each side of the painting. Take off the remaining protective coating on each piece and carefully lower the mat. When you lower the mat, the sides and bottom will adhere as the pieces of Velcro stick together. Each time you raise the mat to remove a painting, the Velcro will part. Without Velcro, the lower edge of the mat will hang loose and away from the backing once it is up on the wall.

Some framing stores will cut both mat and backing for you. However, if you can find an art store or framing shop that has a cutter available for the public (meaning anyone buying the mat board and backing material from them), doing it yourself will cost much less, perhaps as much as two-thirds less. It is wise to economize on your mat, since it is likely to get dirty from frequent handling.

You may find it odd and paradoxical that, having told you to paint with indifference to what is forming on the paper, I am now emphasizing the importance of having a way to display selected paintings. All your paintings are a part of you, and even those you consider horrible should be cared for as a way of acknowledging and respecting all aspects of yourself. Displaying selected paintings honors all of your paintings and your own individuality, as Jo reported in her final summary:

"I was thrilled upon hanging my first Mess Painting and each one thereafter. Even the ones I didn't like initially, I found fascinating and worthwhile once they were hung. Many of my Mess Painting sessions were spent releasing much grief, anger and sadness. Discovering beauty, worthwhileness and inspiration in the paintings which emerged from such pain seemed miraculous and was quite a revelation for me. I found that I am curiously detached from the paintings, distantly intrigued by what emerged from me onto the paper. I have also been quite accepting and non-judgmental toward my paintings. This self-acceptance and lack of harsh criticism is new and feels great. It spills over, too, in my feelings for and acceptance of others."

Whether or not you are reluctant to have others — housemates, family, visitors — see these paintings, you should tell them how important it is for you to hang up paintings you hate as well as those you like. Ask them not to comment on your paintings unless by chance one appeals to them very much. Be sure they understand that joking or negative, non-verbal expressions are not welcome.

Each painting that receives this special treatment should be signed, as an artist would a masterpiece, with your name or initials highly visible in the right-hand corner. When the painting is removed from the mat, it should be placed back in the session in the numerical order where it belongs. Later, any time you review your paintings, the signature will identify it as one you hung on your wall. *Be meticulous about exchanging the paintings every two or three days.* Hang the matted painting in a place where you cannot avoid seeing it frequently when you are at home. The kitchen, bathroom, or above the TV are some possibilities. <u>SELECT MORE PAINTINGS THAT YOU DISLIKE THAN ONES THAT PLEASE YOU!</u>

A great deal of thought and experimentation went into designing the Creativity Mobilization Technique. Using a mat with a backing rather than just tacking your paintings up on a wall has proven to be extremely productive. In fact, some participants have chosen to provide themselves with more than one mat and backing. Looking at your work, particularly those paintings you think are ugly, not only increases self-acceptance but also broadens your perception of what is visually enjoyable.

While you are creating the mat and backing, you probably cannot imagine that it will be exciting to look at your own work. I assure you that it will be. In fact you will often discover that a painting you detested is suddenly fascinating.

As Soetsu Yanagi, the founder of Japan's modern craft movement, remarked: *"Beauty doesn't require prettiness . . . Some pieces of art are not pleasing to look at and yet their content and form are arresting and lure the heart into profound imagination."*

Your own paintings may do that, too.

LIST OF SUPPLIES

You will need to obtain the following items for your setup. (See text box on page 81 for information on where to order paint and brushes.)

	Seven copies of Checklist from Chapter 5
	Drop cloths
	Carpet remnant
	Table or work bench
	Working surface
	Lights: At least two 150-watt bulbs. Preferably one of these should be a full-spectrum 150-watt plant light.
	24 drying trays or more
	Chair or stool
	Paint (water-based tempera): one gallon each of black, white, brown, red, yellow, blue, green and violet (you will probably need more later)
	12 brushes with natural bristles
	8 one-pint plastic containers for paint
	1 or 2 wallpapering troughs, depending on the size of the plastic containers
	Plastic wrap to cover trough
	Wall Street Journals
	Clothespins, giant paper clips, or spring clips for holding the paintings from each session together until your weekly review
	Rags
	Sponge
	Facial tissue or paper towels
	Mat and backing
	Broad felt-tip marking pen
	Loose-leaf notebook and pen
	Notebook for dreams (optional; dreams can be recorded in your loose-leaf binder)
	Water bucket
	Spray bottle (optional)
	Old clothing or painter's coverall and old shoes
	"Do Not Disturb" sign
	Timepiece — large-faced clock or watch with second hand, or an old-fashioned egg timer
	Pine oil, eucalyptus oil, wintergreen oil, or incense (optional)
	Sports bottle of drinking water (optional)
	Electric heater (optional)
	Electric fan (optional)

Chapter Four

Getting Started

"What is important about painting is painting, [not] the doing it right or wrong, good or bad, finished or unfinished."
- Henry Miller

A successful beginning with CMT starts with being sure your work area is as efficient and comfortable as possible. Do you have everything you need at hand? If you are uncertain, take a moment to read through the supply list at the end of Chapter 3. Then, having made any necessary additions to your setup, look at your clock or wristwatch and ask yourself: *"Do I have enough time to paint, to relax afterward, and to record what happened?"* If your answer is not a firm yes, you will do better to postpone the session until evening or the next day.

If you are very impatient to get started, I want to caution you. In your enthusiasm to get on with CMT, you may attempt to paint when it is ill-advised. Rushing through a session, and/or stopping prematurely, will not produce good results.

Do not start or continue painting when your privacy is suddenly violated by the arrival of your mother, housemate, friend, or insurance agent. Even their presence in an adjacent room will probably inhibit you. If a session is interrupted by an unexpected visitor or a household emergency, try to complete it later that same day. Consider these two shorter sessions as one session. Doing two shorter sessions in one day is also recommended if you are ill, or suffering other physical limitations such as severe joint pain.

Last-Minute Preparations

Before you begin, refer to the list of last-minute preparations below. Attending to all of the items listed, *at every painting session,* will help to prevent interruptions during the session. This will help you to avoid undesirable reactions and counterproductive experiences.

LAST-MINUTE PREPARATIONS

• Have you made seven copies of the Checklist in Chapter 5, and do you have it in your work space, along with your Journal and pen?

• Did you clear your calendar of business or personal visitors?

• Is the telephone buried or off the hook?

• Is the radio/TV/CD player shut off?

• Have you put pets where they won't ask for attention?

• Is the "Do Not Disturb" sign on your door?

• Do you have your Checklists, Journal notebook, and pen in your work space? (See Chapter 5.)

• Are you wearing clothes, including shoes or slipper socks, that you don't care about?

• Do you have a jar of hand cream or Vaseline available? Before you start painting you may want to get some protective substance under your nails, around the cuticle, and on the skin of your hands to make cleanup easier. Thoroughly wipe off any excess on the palms of your hands; otherwise, holding on to a brush will be difficult.

(continued)

- Do you have a pail of water, a sponge, and possibly a spray bottle filled with water? You will need water for wetting the work surface, and for discarding a brush to soak in case mental trickery lets you drop your yellow brush into the black paint.

- Do you have some old rags handy? The Department of Self-Sabotage may cause an accident.

- Do you have facial tissue or a towel handy near the working surface? A bit of paint may splash in your eye or on your glasses.

- Do you have a brush in each pot of paint, and some extra brushes nearby?

Work Surface

You will need to wet the work surface with water so that the newspaper won't move around while you are painting. Use a soaked sponge or a spray bottle, or throw handfuls of water on the work surface and then spread it around. Attaching the newspaper with thumb tacks or masking tape would be much more time consuming, and would seriously interrupt the spontaneous flow of the painting process. It would be difficult anyway, once you have started making a mess.

If a few areas of the newspaper are quite wet and the rest are damp, the newspaper will adhere to the working surface and stay in place while you paint. With experience you will know how much water to use. You will need to repeat this wetting process throughout the session. You may wish to wet the board, put paper down, and then lightly spray the paper. It is not a good idea to make the surface so wet that the sheet of newspaper becomes totally saturated when you put it down, because the paper will tend to tear. Also, if you overly wet a newspaper and then load it with paint, you will find it difficult to move onto a drying tray. Be patient and content to learn by trial and error.

Paint will accumulate on your working surface whenever a loaded brush goes beyond the margins of the newspaper. If you are using a fiberboard surface and the edges of the next sheet of newspaper happen to be placed on this wet paint, so much the better. This will help to keep the newspaper in place.

If your working surface is a a Formica countertop, a window, or plywood tightly covered with thin plastic, you should use a large sponge to wet the surface. As you wet the surface in preparation for placing the next sheet of newspaper, any paint left beyond the margins of the last sheet will be wiped away, but the paper will stick to the surface nonetheless.

Always put the newspaper down horizontally, with the bottom edge of the newspaper about two inches from the edge of the working surface. As you take each newspaper from your numbered stack of *Wall Street Journals*, be sure to put it down so that its <u>number is on the back</u> and the <u>print facing you is upside down</u>. Because the numbers are on the back, they will not get covered with paint. Having the print upside down will discourage you from reading the newspaper. If some news item does catch your eye and you really want to read it, put that sheet aside until later and continue painting. After you read the sheet, throw it away. In the long run it is better to have a few numbered sheets missing than to interrupt the painting process.

Hansi, a young counselor-in-training, wrote of her beginning experience: *"Starting CMT took effort and time. Getting all the 'structural' parts of the program into alignment so that the 'process' part could take place was a hassle and was definitely an additional stress in my life. But then what I learned from that is my need to have everything perfect before I can get started on something. Rather than just going with it I tend to put these expectations on myself that I have to meet, so it's no wonder, having this attitude toward things I 'have to do,' that everything I do becomes a pressure like one of those adjustable nozzles on a garden hose. Slowly but surely my need for 'perfection' keeps me tightening the nozzle. Finally I just started. Not everything was perfect but I just plunged in and it was an absolute pleasure."*

If you too are a perfectionist, taking a cue from Hansi's experience may help you get started.

The First Week

The First Painting Session. At some point you will want to record the frustrations, problems, and questions that came up while you gathered your supplies and set up your space. Right now, with the last-minute preparations accomplished, the wetting of the work surface taken care of, and the paper in place, close your eyes, take a deep breath, go inside yourself and see what's happening physically and emotionally. Are you excited, apprehensive, relaxed, tired, or irritated? Are you looking forward to painting? Write down in your Journal whatever you just observed.

You may not want to take the time before you begin this first painting session to write down all your reactions to the task of setting up your painting space; but be sure to record these feelings and thoughts in your Journal during your first week of painting. Chapter 5 gives full instructions on the important record-keeping component of CMT. I am assuming you have read it and made copies of the Checklist before starting to paint.

In general the way anyone paints is influenced by how they are feeling. The instructions that follow are based on the assumption that at this moment, as you are poised, brush in hand, you are feeling more or less okay. Perhaps you are a bit apprehensive about starting something new, but you are not about to burst into tears or explode with anger. If by chance you are in an intense emotional state, you should do what you can to paint how you feel. If you have already read through this book as recommended, you may want to reread the story of Eleanor's stormy first session in Chapter 6 (pages 154-155) before proceeding.

It is very important that several times, during this and the next few sessions, you check on how long you are spending on individual paintings. Look at your timepiece just before you pick up a brush to begin painting, and again when you are about to move the painting onto a drying tray. Did you spend one minute, one and a half minutes, two minutes, or longer?

Some people easily cover ninety percent of the paper in a minute and a half. The pace of others is about two minutes. Either is fine, but if you discover that you are going faster or slower, see what adjustments you can make in the rhythm of your brush strokes.

Remember, you are not making art. You are simply getting acquainted with your tools — your brushes, paint, and paper — and training your time sense.

Begin by trying out all sorts of brush strokes — slow, fast, short, long. See what happens when you use your brush to daub at the paper or to hit the paper as hard as you can. Scoop up gobs of paint on a brush, and before it is all applied on the paper put it back and reach for another brush loaded with paint of a different color. When you are faced with the pale gray of a page of stock prices, take a brush with almost no paint on it, spread the bristles and see the effect as you drag the dry brush across the paper.

If you can't resist getting your fingers into thick areas of colorful paint, fine. See what happens when you push the paint around with your fingernails.

While you are painting, if the yellow brush picks up some previously applied black paint, do not stop to clean it. Just put the now slightly dirty yellow brush back in its container. If doing that goes counter to your child-hood training or your aesthetic sense, be sure to complain in your Journal about how you hate having the colors get dirty.

If a brush falls on the floor, do not stop to clean it. Throw the brush in your handy pail of water and use one of your extra brushes. Not cleaning brushes during the painting session is a must.

Paint with only one brush at a time, and paint with your dominant hand. Do not use two hands. If you were born left-handed but trained to use your right hand, use your left. If you are ambidextrous, choose the hand you would play tennis with. If you still are not sure which hand to use, paint at least fifteen consecutive paintings with one hand, and the next session (pref-erably the next day) paint another fifteen consecutive paintings with the other hand. You will know which hand to use in the future by the way it feels.

What forms can you create with your brushes? As you more or less cover one of your numbered newspapers after another, try making zigzags, grids, big intertwining spirals, large elliptical shapes, circles, squares, triangles, or rainbows. Use all the colors on some paintings, and very few on others. Blanket the paper with one color before adding any others. Paint flowers, houses, trees, fish, birds, faces.

Become like a four-year-old when you paint, and reach for any color. If you paint a landscape, who cares if the ground is red or the sky is yellow? If you paint faces, who cares if the eyes are the same size, or if a brush loaded with violet dirties a bright green area? Experiment. Find out what colors you prefer, and which combinations please you the most. If the idea of painting recognizable shapes puts you off, do whatever you like. The idea is to get started.

When you have covered about ninety percent of the newspaper, lift up the bottom edge of the painting, slide one of your drying trays underneath it, and pull the painting further onto the tray. Then place this tray down on the floor — nearby, but not in the way. Or you can put the drying tray down on the floor first and, holding two corners of the painting, lift it off the working surface and place it on the drying tray on the floor. Either way, next put a riser (a cup) at each corner of the drying tray in order to support the next drying tray and its painting. Repeat this process until the first stack is about twelve trays high, and then start another stack. When the stacks get too high, they wobble and tend to fall over.

After placing the first painting to dry, quickly wet your work surface, place the number two sheet of *The Wall Street Journal* on it, and immediately start painting again.

At first you may feel some tension in painting, so please take it easy. In the first session if nine or ten paintings seem enough for you, then stop. Don't pressure yourself to do the suggested fifteen to twenty. You are looking for a sense of completion, not fatigue. Painting to the point of exhaustion is not beneficial. Later in the week you will find it easy to do more.

When you finish painting, if the paint in your containers is low then drop your brushes in the pail of water. You needn't stop to clean them now unless you prefer to do so; later will do just as well. Never leave the brushes in the paint containers overnight if the bristles aren't completely covered with paint. Cover the containers with plastic wrap.

Now ask yourself what you want to do next. Take a hot tub or shower? Meditate? Go for a walk? Nap?

Right after painting you may choose to fill out your Checklist and write in your Journal any observations that need greater detail, or that were not covered in the Checklist. Or you may prefer to do the Journal writing later on, after relaxing. Just be sure to do so before you go to sleep for the night.

If you had a good time during your first session, if you enjoyed exploring the suggestions about how and what to paint, you may not have a great deal to report. But, since we all know there are an infinite number of words for expressing dislike and comparatively few for expressing pleasure, you may find you have more to record if your initial experience was as difficult as John's:

"When I first set out to undertake this adventure I experienced ambivalent feelings. A part of me felt overwhelmed by the structure and details of the process, while another part of me was ready to create and to paint. When I started painting the process seemed awkward, clumsy and foreign. The less-than-two-minute time limit felt rushed and hurried. My whole world seemed under pressure."

Recording your responses to the instructions is essential. Your reactions to the difficulties inherent in CMT will mirror how you handle things in other situations and provide you with valuable insight.

The Second Painting Session. As you enter your work space to do your next or any other session, your initial concern will be whether or not the paintings have dried. If there are only a few damp places on two or three paintings, just cover these spots with pieces of wax paper as you stack the paintings. If the paintings are very wet, you will need to find some other way to continue to dry them.

You can spread out the still-wet paintings on the garage floor, or on an old bed sheet or a plastic drop cloth placed somewhere in your living space. If you wish to lay the paintings outside to finish drying, be sure to put rocks on the corners; otherwise, any breeze will send them flying. If the paint is not so wet that it will run or drip off the paper, you could use a clothesline and clothespins, but there are disadvantages to this solution. The paintings are apt to dry unevenly, with the edges drying much faster than the center and curling up so they become difficult to stack or put in your mat. They will also be hard to deal with when you review them at the end of the week.

Some people have coped with this problem by ironing the curled-up paintings flat. If you decide to do this, put a large piece of plain brown wrapping paper on the ironing board or on a carpeted floor. Place each one of your paintings on the brown wrapping paper with the painted side down. Using a spray bottle, lightly moisten the back of the painting with water before ironing. This will help the painting respond to the hot iron and flatten out.

To avoid the extra effort of dealing with paintings that haven't dried fast enough, consider improving the air flow around your drying trays by keeping a window open. Better yet, use an electric heater or fan. Don't put it too close to the stack of drying trays — not only to guard against fire, but also to allow the paintings to dry evenly, without curling up at the edges.

After removing the paintings from the first session, stack your drying trays on edge once again. This is a good time to select a painting for display in your mat. Remember to select paintings you don't like as well as those you do. Be sure to sign any painting you place in your mat.

Please continue to follow the instructions given earlier on pages 96 and 97 about making sure you have enough time both to paint and to relax afterward, stopping if your privacy is violated, attending to last-minute preparations, placing the newspaper on the wet work surface, drying and storing the paintings, and journaling.

Now, as at the first painting session, before beginning write a few words in your Journal about how you are feeling at this moment. Today, I suggest that you pick up one of your extra brushes. Hold it as you would a stick you have found on the beach, with which you intend to draw something in the wet sand. All the fingers should be touching the handle of the brush, not just two or three of them as in holding a writing pen.

Close your eyes, put your attention on the back of your neck and on both shoulders, take a deep breath, and say slowly: *"My neck and shoulders are heavy."* Keep repeating this slowly and breathing deeply, until you feel your shoulders drop.

Open your eyes and, staying relaxed, paint in the air. Imagine that the brush is a wand you are waving. Bend the elbow freely, but not the wrist. Use the arm/hand/brush as a unit, and see how many ways you can move it around. Use large arm movements as much as possible. Which of the various movements you have just explored does your arm prefer to make today? One day your arm may choose somewhat vertical motions, while on another they will tend to be more horizontal, perhaps mixed with diagonals or partial figure eights.

Put the dry brush down and grab a brush from one of your pots of glistening paint. The best thing to do, unless you feel a strong emotional need for a certain color or colors, is to use the colors randomly.

If the exercise with breath and brush feels awkward and you don't want to practice it you will need to find something else to help you get started. It is a problem most painters face, about which Henry Miller wrote:

"One is apt to begin consciously using one's head, not one's intuitive feeling. Consequently the first two or three are abortions and I throw them on the floor... and then I become nervous, even frantic, for the light is already fading and the dinner bell will soon ring. Now I shut off the thinking machine, or more properly, the worrying machine. Full steam ahead and the devil take the hindmost! If I happen to put my brush into red paint I begin with red; if blue, then it's blue. What difference does it make? To begin is the thing, begin anywhere, anyhow. So it goes. What results is not of my bidding. It's either the work of the devil or my guardian angel!"[1]

If you hum, whistle and sing nonsense words as you stack your dry paintings and fill your paint pots, that may set the stage to turn off your thinking machine and let your arm/hand/brush do its dance. Push, sweep, stroke onto the newspaper one brush full of paint after another. Always drop each brush back in its container before all the paint on it has been laid down. Let your brush strokes go beyond the margins of the paper. You will find it exhilarating to go beyond the "lines," as you were forbidden to do in your coloring books when you were a child. This will also help you to loosen up or get rid of other limiting rules you still carry from your childhood. Gay Luce, in *Your Second Life*, wrote in her chapter on CMT: *"Ultimately if you can indulge in spontaneous Mess Painting you can liberate yourself from the rules that interfere with your own creativity."*

Many of the things you may have done while becoming familiar with the materials are a big "no-no" when you are attempting to Mess Paint. Rainbowing, filling in all the empty spaces, blanketing the paper with one color before adding any others, painting identifiable forms, or making borders, to mention a few, are to be avoided. Clean areas of color must give way to a confusion of overlapping brush strokes. You will also need to resist imitating what you think a Mess Painting looks like.

Spattering may happen by chance and be part of the general freedom of your brush work. On occasion it may be the final exuberant gesture or delicate flip of delight. Get rid of spattering as an aesthetic choice; however, the spattering that occurs spontaneously because you are angrily hitting the paper with the brush is fine. Spattering in this case comes about because of acting out emotions and is not part of consciously making a painting more interesting. If you loved spattering and want to do more, you will soon have the opportunity to experiment with spatter painting at the end of your Mess Painting sessions (see Chapter 7).

Go back and forth between colors, alternating with each brushful. It is not necessary to use all eight colors in any one painting. Most of the time, three or four will be sufficient. Occasionally you may find it necessary to paint with only one or two colors to express your emotional needs.

Part of the trick in learning to create Mess Paintings is to get to a mental state where you really don't care about making aesthetic choices of colors.

You are no longer to concern yourself with what looks pretty or interesting. Going for a color because it corresponds to a gut-level emotion is not the same as wanting the colors to look lovely next to each other on the paper.

RULES FOR MESS PAINTING

- Hold the brush like a wand, not a pencil.
- Choose colors at random, or in response to your emotional needs.
- Alternate colors with each brushful of paint, generally using three or four colors, but breaking this rule as your feeling guides you..
- Use full arm movements.
- Allow brush strokes to overlap.
- Paint beyond the edges of the paper.
- Use vocalization and gestures to express emotion as you paint.
- Cover approximately ninety percent of the page.
- Paint no longer than two minutes on any painting, usually a little less.

Jane described in her final summary how she let go of aesthetic considerations in her paintings: *"I began by painting out a lot of my feelings, especially my rage, pain, hurt, grief. I also was very aware of not wanting any painting to have to look 'pretty,' so I systematically slashed out and painted over any vestiges of aesthetic pleasure. I felt very rebellious, and through my acts of defiance I felt like I was saying to the world, 'I don't have to do it the way you want it. I don't have to be pretty, bright, perfect, or right for you. I can make it any way I want, including ugly and undesirable and wrong in your judgment!'"*

Spontaneous no-thought Mess Paintings do not happen if you are paying close attention to the act of painting. You can't watch yourself and at the same time let go of any expectations. So side-step your anxiety about doing it right.

Between sessions, change the position of the paint containers in the trough to help avoid the automatic over-use of certain colors. Put the colors in a different order each time — one day have black in the center and easiest to reach; the next day put it at one end of the trough where it is harder to reach. Rearrange all the colors in this way.

As in the first session, don't worry about completing fifteen or twenty paintings. If doing twelve seems enough, quit at that point, but be sure to jot down your thoughts about terminating the session. For instance, did you stop too soon? Do you feel left with "unfinished business?" Among your other observations in your Journal, record how this session went as compared with your thoughts and feelings in the first session.

If you choose to continue to just experiment with the materials in your second session, that's fine. There is no set rule about how many sessions of conscious experimentation with materials to do before attempting Mess Painting. For purposes of helping you evaluate your paintings, I will assume that in the first week you have done at least one and possibly two sessions following the guidelines for Mess Painting.

Reviewing the Painting Sessions from Week One

A day or so after finishing three or four sessions, it is time to have a look at them.

Before examining the paintings, take a moment to congratulate yourself. You have completed an enormous task. You now own a work space. You bought your supplies, gathered together everything you needed, and arranged it all in a place where you could be alone. You explored the possibilities of the colors and the brush work, got acquainted with school tempera paint, wrote in your Journal, and may have had some fun. You also got a feel for the prescribed time allotment of "no more than two minutes" for each painting.

This is a lot to accomplish. Give yourself a pat on the back.

Next, pause and ask yourself if you did anything this week that you haven't done in a long time, or have never done before. It is not likely that noticeable changes will have occurred so quickly, but this is an important question to ask yourself each week, or sometimes even each day. Please record your observations in your Journal.

Be sure that all the paintings are dry when you review them. Then stack them, *in the right order* (the order they were painted in), with session number one on top followed by session two, then three, then four. Place a labeled, plain piece of newspaper at the top of each session, so that as you review the paintings now, and again at the end of the seven weeks, you can easily see where one session ended and another began.

It is important not only to look at all of the paintings in the exact order in which you painted them, with each session clearly separated from the previous one, but also to be sure you are not looking at the paintings upside down. You want to look at them the way they were painted. If you always paint with the print upside down, it will be very easy to stack the paintings correctly.

Have you placed a painting in your mat? Remember to put it back in the session exactly where it belongs.

Now take the stack of paintings from the first session and place it on a table so that you can turn the sheets of newspaper as though you were reading a book. Be sure there is adequate illumination, and that you have a chair handy in case you want to sit down to read your notes. You will probably need to stand to view the paintings.

Try to look at each painting dispassionately. Simply notice whether you made zigzags, spirals, grids, circles, triangles, squares, rectangles, polka dots, or other forms. Did you fill in large areas? Did you do a lot of spattering? Did you blanket the newspaper with one color before using another? Did you paint a border on one or more sides of the paper? Did you have fun choosing which colors to put together? Did any of your paintings have recognizable content, i.e., buildings, faces, trees, flowers, birds, fish? What sort of self-talk went on? How many were very messy?

All of the paintings you have done so far (even those that look messy to you) probably are not "Mess Paintings." One way to determine this is to check through and see if the appearance of each painting differs from the others. The more unique each one is, the more you can be certain you were not doing spontaneous Mess Painting. In my view the greater variety you have created this first week the better, even though this variety indicates a greater focus on what you are doing than occurs in Mess Painting. Particularly for persons who are inexperienced with art materials, it is important to create as much variety as possible during the introductory period. This helps to build a repertoire of possibilities to try during the following weeks, when you are encouraged to do a couple of playful Experimental Paintings at the end of most Mess Painting sessions (see Chapter 7).

In the one or two painting sessions of this first week where you set out to make Mess Paintings, how similar were these paintings to each other in use of color and patterns of brush work? If you can find a sequence of four or five paintings that are equally dark or light, and if each of these paintings has approximately the same amount of, say, blue, black, and brown, or whatever colors you chose, then you are well on your way to experiencing Mess Painting.

On the other hand, if in reviewing the paintings from what you intended to be a Mess Painting session, you see a dark messy painting followed by a light painting, or a blue, black, and white one followed by a yellow, green, and white one, you can assume that you were still experimenting with the materials when you created them. As you review your Checklist and Journal notes along with the paintings, you may discover that during the session you were anxious or indulged in self-criticism. This would be further evidence that you were not in a state of flow that allows spontaneous Mess Painting to happen.

Please be sure to check whether or not you painted beyond the edges of the newspaper. Not doing so is probably the most common error of beginning Mess Painters, the one that I have found myself pointing out to clients over and over again during the first few two or three weeks.

After looking at all the paintings and concomitantly reading your Journal notes, give yourself a symbolic gold star. If your notes show that you spent time alone after painting — relaxing and reflecting while taking a hot bath, stretching out on your bed, going for a walk, or meditating — congratulations. You deserve another gold star. Give yourself a third gold star for all the effort you have put out so far in this project of self-renewal.

The demands that CMT makes — namely, to do four painting sessions each week, to fill out Checklists and write in your Journal and take time afterwards for reflection — are considerable. Arranging sufficient time for CMT will probably be difficult. You may need to curtail social engagements, TV viewing, or other activities. Most of us tend to fill our lives with excessive stimulation. Our ears are not physiologically capable of listening to the noise level of most rock bands or of loud industrial machinery without suffering permanent hearing loss. In the same way, our inner healer is not able to maintain physical and psychological equilibrium with the excessive busy-ness that we impose upon ourselves or allow to be imposed on us by others. Certainly this busy-ness does not allow for spiritual growth. We may think it will be easy to just add on CMT to the rest of what we have promised ourselves or others that we would do.

Susan was one of the many who had this expectation. In her Journal she described the disparity between her expectations and what actually happened:

"I hoped CMT would (magically?) relieve me of something — of what? A sense of burden and struggle with life? I hoped that I would be able to see my way through the obstacles I erect and feel in my life.

"I expected CMT to do all the work. I expected this thing outside of me to magically do something — to improve my life in a way similar, say, to what I imagined receiving a million dollars would do. Strangely enough, despite all of Virginia's detailed instructions for setting up and getting started, I didn't expect ME to do the work. For instance, I never thought I would learn to use a mat cutter. When I imagined doing CMT, I had just a lovely picture of me painting with lots of time and joy of artistic creativity! Never was there an image in my head of a lot of shit and struggle."

Accept whatever time it takes for your system to shift and fall into "letting go" while you paint. In my experience, everyone who manages to shift priorities, stick with the time demands, and follow the instructions of CMT has very satisfying results. Perhaps it is a push from their inner child — or maybe it's just plain stubbornness — that gets people through all the initial difficulties and into enjoying the whole painting process.

---

[1]Henry Miller, "To Paint Is to Love Again," in *The Paintings of Henry Miller: Essays by Henry Miller*, Chronicle Books, 1982.

Chapter Five

Record Keeping

> *"I don't know in advance what I am going to put on the canvas, any more than I decide in advance what colors to use. Whilst I work, I take no stock of what I am painting on the canvas. Every time I begin a picture, I feel as though I were throwing myself into the void. I never know if I shall land on my feet again. It is only later than I begin to evaluate the results of my work."*
> - Pablo Picasso

I am delighted that so renowned an artist as Pablo Picasso has described the painting process as he does above. Picasso's description of his state of consciousness while painting strongly resembles the state I have identified with "letting go" and "optimal experience." Note that Picasso makes a distinction between the act of painting and that of evaluation. For Mess Painters as for Picasso, evaluation is a separate activity. In the case of CMT it is facilitated by record keeping.

Unlike Picasso, many artists habitually mix up the creative act of painting, writing, or composing with the act of evaluation. Most of the people I work with, artists and non-artists alike, are initially so concerned about how others may judge them or their paintings that they *contaminate the act of creation with their own critical thoughts.* As long as they maintain this self-critical attitude they miss out on the revitalization and release that come from painting in a state of flow.

Generally when visual artists evaluate their professional work they are concerned with technical details such as composition, texture, integrity of line, relationship of colors and forms; then, finally, they assess the *emotional impact of the painting*. It is this last consideration that most keenly interests Mess Painters, who are primarily concerned with the *process* of painting, with how a painting stimulates or reflects their sensations and emotions.

A group of Oakland artists known as The Society of Six had as their credo: *"We do not believe that painting is a language. Nor do we try to 'say' things, but we do try to fix upon canvas the joy of vision. . . . We have much to express but nothing to say. We have felt, and desire that others may also feel."*

Similarly, Mess Painters are pleased when their work fully expresses the emotions they were feeling while painting, and are often surprised that others are affected emotionally as they view the same paintings.

The Checklist

In order to help you keep a record of your thoughts, emotions, and sensations while painting, the CMT process includes written records of three types — the Journal, the Checklist, and the Dream Diary. You were briefly introduced to Journal writing in Chapter 4. Before I expand on the Journal, let me introduce the Checklist you will use at each painting session.

The Checklist is a convenient tool for recording and comparing the details of what happened in your painting sessions. Begin a new Checklist each week. At the beginning of the week, write in your name and the number of the week (1, 2, 3, etc.).

At the end of each painting session, you have the choice of recording what happened immediately, or of doing so a little later after spending some time with yourself bathing, walking, meditating, or just relaxing.

When you start recording, fill in the numbers of the paintings just completed — for example, #1 to #15, or #39 to #65 — rather than the total number you have just created. At the next session the numbers will begin where the last left off, in this case with #16 or # 66.

Keeping track of the hour of the day and the day of the week is also important. Later, when you are reviewing your work at the end of each week and at final review, you will want to know if sessions were spaced close together, one day after another, or if there was a long interval following a particular session. Your Journal notes will help clarify whether an outside event interfered, or whether something about the painting session itself caused you to back off and postpone the next painting encounter.

The heading of your checklist should look something like this:

Full Name: ___*Mary Doe*___   Week No. *1*

SESSION #	1	2	3	4	(5)
Painting Identification Numbers	1/15	16/36	37/51	52/70	
Time of Day	6AM	7AM	5PM	11AM	
Date or Day of the Week	Mon	Thurs	Fri	Sat	

Next, take your time and record as accurately as possible what happened to you while painting. You can fill out the Checklist for each painting session, or incorporate your answers into your Journal notes. Please keep in mind that it is very unlikely that any one person would experience every sensation, emotion, or behavior in the list during the course of the entire program.

The Checklist is not to be considered the final authority on what might take place. You may need to write in additional words to describe accurately the physical sensations, feelings, or thoughts that you had. If you were singing or humming a specific song, write down its name, or the words. If you had physical sensations or reactions that are not listed on the Checklist, write them in. No matter how unusual or odd some of your responses may seem to you, remember that they are evidence that your self-regulating mechanisms are working on your behalf. A backache may be telling you that your table height is not right, or it could be a sign of a need to cry. A brief, sharp pain in your forearm might be related to the pain you suffered as a child when you fell from a tree and broke a bone. Any twinge of pain may be an indication that your body is dealing with something that happened in the past. Be patient and accepting of these odd sensations, so that they can be resolved and leave.

You can expect the variety, frequency and intensity of your reactions to wax and wane. Moreover, many of your sensations and feelings will probably not reach the level of conscious awareness. *Do not assume that nothing happened within you simply because nothing was felt* .

In using the Checklist, I recommend that you quantify your answers. A simple check mark tells you very little. Later on, when reviewing all of your notes along with the paintings, you will be grateful for the added information that a one-to-five scale provides for each observed response. It will remind you, for example, whether you cried very briefly or copiously, and enable you to compare more accurately how one session differed from another.

If you make a financial arrangement with me to review your paintings and your written records, it is essential that you fill out the Checklists. You will need to send these to me as part of the written record of your painting experience (see Epilogue).

Permission is given to photocopy the following five Checklist pages. Please make seven (or more) copies, one for each week, and keep them in the loose-leaf binder that you use for your Journal. Be sure to enlarge each page to 8 ¹/₂" by 11" — about 115 percent. You may find you'll want to add a few additional lines to the columns. If you are singing many songs you can record them in your Journal or write them on the back of the Checklist. Also copy the Checklist Rating Scale, found on page 117, for handy reference.

AFTER THE PAINTINGS ARE DRY YOU ARE ENCOURAGED TO LOOK AT THEM. The ones you select to place in your mat may relate to some specific moment in the session, or may be chosen because you particularly like or dislike them. Remember to sign those you select.

CHECKLIST RATING SCALE

Keep this scale handy as you fill out the Checklist.

0 = not observed during the painting period
(leave the space <u>blank</u>)

1 = occasionally, fleetingly, once or twice

2 = sometimes, moderately, three to six times

3 = frequently, prominently, seven or more times

4 = a lot, very intensely

5 = almost continuously

CMT CHECKLIST

Full Name: _____ Week No._____

SESSION #	1	2	3	4	(5)
Painting Identification Numbers					
Time of Day					
Date or Day of the Week					

WHILE I WAS PAINTING . . .

	1	2	3	4	(5)
time passed very quickly					
time passed very slowly					
nothing special happened with time					
I felt muscle tension					
I had a backache					
I had a headache					
I had cramps or spasms					
I had abdominal pains					
I had other pain (Where?)					
I clenched my jaw					
I ground my teeth					
I made dance-like movements					
I used the brushes aggressively					
I made gestures					
I yawned					
I hummed					
I sang (What song?)					
I whistled					
I grimaced					
I laughed					
I sobbed					
I cried					
I coughed					
I spit					
I perspired					
I retched, gagged					
I vomited					
I talked (non-aggressively)					
I was verbally aggressive					
I cursed, used profanities					
I shouted					
I talked baby talk					
I made nonsense sounds					
I grunted					
I made animal noises					
I groaned					

WHILE PAINTING I FELT:

pleasure				
satisfaction				
frustration				
irritation				
boredom				
sexual arousal				
infantile feelings				
helplessness				
sense of flow				
surprise				
change in body image				
"empty" mental silence				
anger				
rage				
ecstasy				
hungry				
thirsty				
lonely				
frightened				
imprisoned, claustrophobic				
anxious				
ridiculous				
critical				
a need for more air				
a lump in my throat				
tearing of my eyes				
shivering				
trembling				
electricity-like tingling				
dizziness				
exhaustion				
normal fatigue				
relief, recuperation				
revitalization, rejuvenation				
depression				
sadness				
impatience				
joy				
comfort				

WHILE PAINTING I FELT A:

need to: rest more					
increase physical activity					
talk to certain persons					
change certain behavior					
change my lifestyle					
change certain attitudes					
go on a vacation					
need for: greater independence					
more self-affirmation					
more social contact					
solitude					
freedom					
need for more self-expression . . . in music					
in writing					
in art					
in dance					
in home decorating					
in talking with others					
other					

Please make a check mark (✓) where appropriate, instead of the usual 1-5 judgment.

JUST AFTER I FINISHED PAINTING, I FELT:

same as before					
better					
very tired					
refreshed					
anxious					
tense					
relaxed					
euphoric					
happy					
satisfied					
disappointed					
agitated					
disturbed					
Termination was: probably correct					
perhaps premature					
not sure					

Please make a check mark (✓) where appropriate.

LATER WHILE RELAXING (a nice bath is highly recommended):

I felt nothing special					
I had many ideas					
I had specific memories					
I made decisions					
I made plans					
I looked at myself in a mirror (try this!)					
I was humming					
I was singing					
I was whistling					
I was playful					
I was caressing my body					
I felt a need for love, nurturing, sex					
I had no special interest in my body					
I felt more interest in my body than usual					
I made plans for body care					

Body messages. You may have noticed that many of the items in the Checklist refer to body sensations, body functions and body movements. The observations of CMT painters demonstrate that when change is actually happening one can sense it in the body. *This is not just getting in touch with feelings.* It is the body sensed inwardly, as it carries what isn't yet clear mentally about a problem or an interpersonal situation.

Being aware of the nuances of sensations in your body gives you important clues for happier, healthier living, just as paying attention to intuition does. One of the benefits of doing this painting process is that CMT makes many people more sensitive to body sensations, and these physical sensations often occur before you have mentally identified the associated emotion. If we are able to tune in to body sensations — for instance, to a queasy tummy suggesting that something in a situation is not right — then we have more information to guide us in our everyday choices.

The Journal

Some Mess Painters dislike checklists. They prefer to read through the Checklist from time to time and, keeping the items in mind, include the information in their Journal entries. Extensive Journal writing is a satisfying activity for many Mess Painters, while others prefer using the Checklist because it simplifies and shortens what they need to record in their Journal.

As you learned in Chapter 4, your Journal begins at Session 1 of Week 1 with your hopes and fears — your expectations around CMT — and your reactions to the task of setting up a work space. After each session, I urge you to document as much as possible of what was going on while you were painting and immediately after. What were you thinking about your life, about your unfulfilled needs? What were you feeling? While painting, what was going on in your body? How did you move, and use the brush? Were you hitting or slapping the paper? Were you crying, moaning, laughing? These observations, if they are not recorded in your Checklist, should be entered in your Journal soon after painting if possible, or at least later the same day.

Your Journal notes should also include your reactions, session by session, to the colors — your emotional responses to them, and how much of each color you used. You may detest black during a painting session, but at the same time you may need to use a lot of black because its unpleasantness fits with the thoughts and images surfacing in your consciousness. Your paintings will be out of sight on the drying trays as you do your record keeping, so you won't know exactly how much of each color you actually used. Just give a *quick guess;* then later when you are reviewing the paintings you can see whether you did indeed use a lot of black, for instance, or whether your dislike and/or fear of black won out over your need to use it.

Monitoring behavioral and attitude change. Keeping track of relevant events that happen between sessions makes it possible to do periodic assessments of the impact of CMT on your life. Did you resume an activity you have not engaged in for years? Did you do something you have never done before? Discontinue a troublesome habit, or handle an interpersonal situation differently? A good time to record these between-session events is as you make your Journal entries before you begin painting. Just before you begin to paint, also write down how you are feeling as you are about to start the session.

It is important to pay attention to the paradoxes, problems, and questions that arise both while painting and between sessions. Do you resist or try to circumvent the instructions? Do you feel impatient or frustrated? Does your perfectionism recoil at making a mess?

While you may not find it pleasant to confront habitual patterns of behavior that you know are not in your best interest, spelling out such realizations in your Journal will increase your awareness of them. *Simple awareness, unaccompanied by negative self-talk, will promote positive change.*

When my CMT groups look at their paintings together at the weekly meeting, some people may choose to read some parts of their Journal and Dream Diary out loud. Or, after a silent review of their notes, they may say as much as they feel comfortable sharing about each session and the day-by-day events that relate to the issues that surfaced while painting. I review each person's Checklist, but I certainly do not read anyone's Journal. The Journal is a private place for an ongoing dialogue with oneself, and the contents should be seen only by its author.

Rereading your Journal, not only at the end of the seven-week program (see Epilogue), but also six months or a year later, will enable you to see the long-term results of your CMT program. Not all of the beneficial effects of CMT may be evident until months have gone by.

Marilyn did ten weeks of CMT with me on an individual basis. Some six months after she had completed five hundred and forty-two paintings, she chose to send me her then-current observations on the effect the program had had on her life:

"CMT has made real changes in my life. They are profound yet subtle enough that I didn't realize they were occurring until after I completed the training. Time and again I become aware, 'Oh, there it is again.' What I mean by that is that I find myself saying 'Yes'— Yes to new experiences and opportunities; Yes, when help is offered; Yes to things I would have postponed or rejected — would have rejected even though they were good for me.

"As an example, even though I heard about it too late to attend the first meeting, I took the last three days of a four-day class anyhow. It was on early childhood education, and being held in conjunction with the exhibit of children's artwork from a school in northern Italy.

"I know that in the past I would not have pursued the class since I had missed one day. And I probably would not have gone to the exhibit. I'm a surgical nurse and I don't have any idea of what I'll do with what I am learning. I do know that I am very excited about the concepts guiding this school and seeing the children's art.

"Another shift has been a loosening of my reluctance to sing or make sounds. One of my Experimental Paintings was a precursor to that change." (See Illustration 11, page 130.)

John Curry, an artist, also recognized behavioral changes, as well as changes in his approach to his work:

"CMT seems to simmer in me, and then much later something new happens that I definitely attribute to that process. For example: although after my 1988 experience with CMT I had an incredibly productive year — three one-man shows and several group shows — I didn't begin to use the model in a new way until 1992. Instead of having the model pose and taking photographs of various positions, I hired someone who was a dancer and asked her to dance to music. While watching her, I just let my pencil meander around on the paper.

"What I'm doing now doesn't have to go anywhere other than express my emotional state. The more I do this, the less I am worried about the product. This is true whether it's a painting, drawing, or sculpture. But when I start thinking about the product, the piece goes to hell. I get frustrated. I get angry. I get into all my past habits, old patterns.

"My work is like a life map. How I am is how the piece turns out. So when I look at my work I can see where I was less worried about the finished painting, the finished drawing. Whenever I can get into that state where while painting or sculpting I just process — without a goal — it's indescribable. I don't know how I could have gone on for so many years without understanding this.

"Another thing that gradually came out of CMT was being more able to take risks. Possibly the biggest risk I've ever taken was deciding to close our successful ceramic business and renovate the buildings on our property into elegant fully furnished bed-and-breakfast units, with the idea that once they were built and occupied, we could devote more of our time to being artists.

"After finishing the cottages (which took many months of hard physical work), as I got back into my studio work I felt blocked. When I started to draw, I couldn't. What I was doing was awful. Suddenly I had a vision, or more accurately a hallucination. A piece of newspaper appeared in front of me. I was painting away — feeling how that had felt when I was Mess Painting. And I began to draw in that same state of 'no-mind.'

"Since then I'm usually able to be free as I work. I guess that momentary flashback integrated what I had learned years before in CMT. For instance, when

I take a sponge and erase a whole painting, it's okay. I don't have to save anything. I know the well won't run dry — my creativity won't run out. It seems to me that my latest paintings express the freedom I first discovered in Mess Painting."

The Dream Diary

Another part of record keeping is the Dream Diary. Luthe saw dreaming as a mechanism for maintaining psychological and physiological harmony. He thought the brain produces dreams to reorganize and neutralize events of the day, and that one function of sleep was to permit the brain to do this work. He advocated the same attitude of acceptance toward dreams that he called for in the painting process, and believed that all kinds of dreams should

> *"We all dream in a regular and predictable way every night of our lives, whether we are upset or not. And we usually dream for periods as long as one hour without waking up. In a normal life span of 70 years, an individual devotes at least 50,000 hours to dreaming: that is 2,000 days or six full years of dream time. Dreaming must, therefore, be not only psychologically intriguing but biologically important."*
> - J. Allan Hobson, *The Dreaming Brain*

be welcomed, nightmares included. Luthe believed that keeping a Dream Diary encouraged dream recall and served to acknowledge, honor, and promote this self-regulating, self-healing mechanism of the brain. Luthe stressed encouragement and acceptance of dreaming, rather than dream interpretation.

One of the reasons for recording dreams during the time you are involved with CMT is to experience the relationship between your dreams and the painting sessions. Most Mess Painters report being more conscious of seeing color in their dreams, and some experience brilliant and rapidly changing color patterns.

When a painting session is too short, the brain may produce a frightening dream that night. I suspect that if the brain begins to reorganize some material during the painting session and is unable to complete this self-healing process, it may produce a nightmare simply as a continuation of what began while painting. The nightmare could be, in part, a message telling the dreamer to paint as long as is necessary.

Georgianne, a young ballet teacher, recognized the connection between dreams and Mess Painting when she wrote of one of her sessions: *"I woke up from a realistic dream of violence feeling overwhelmed, heavy, tragic, terribly burdened. Went to my shed to paint soon after waking up and went right for the red and the black. I could not tolerate purple and brown. I felt a physical necessity to do these paintings and used aggressive hard strokes. I kept yelling 'Bitch!' and finally broke my red paint brush from hitting so hard. Afterwards I felt a great sense of relief and years younger. Returned to the house feeling light and eager to see my husband and baby. I realized that I had avoided dealing with aggressive material on the previous day — had cut the painting session short."*

Dreams can also indicate how the painting process is progressing. I remember a woman who reported three similar dreams on three separate nights, with painting sessions in between. In each dream she was in a rowboat on a lake. In the first dream there were no oars; in the second the oars were there but the paddle ends were broken off; in the third the oars were intact, and the dreamer rowed her boat ashore.

Another Mess Painter who experienced the relationship between painting and dreaming is Claire, a teacher in an urban public high school. Claire was still mourning the loss through arson of her family's historic log cabin in the Sierra foothills. Before the fire she had been looking forward to the time when she could retire to this much-loved place in the country.

As she began to let go into Mess Painting, Claire had frequent nightmares about the fire. Coincidentally, all of her repetitious paintings had the colors and almost the form of bonfires in them. It was clear that her need to dream and to paint this way had finally been satisfied when, at the end of two weeks, her paintings changed to a full line of cool colors and her dreams were no longer nightmarish.

As a CMT guide, I do not attempt to *interpret* dreams. Rather I focus on supporting non-judgmental attitudes toward dreaming — acceptance of any kind of material, no matter how crazy, distasteful, frightening, or ugly it may be. I urge my clients to say to themselves before going to sleep, *"Dear brain, I welcome all kinds of dreams. Express whatever you wish; I will not interfere."*

It appears possible that by following this suggestion one can change an ongoing dream pattern. Fran, a gracious, humorous woman in her late sixties, was experiencing a great deal of anger in her painting sessions. For many months she had also been frequently awakened by a frightening nightmare of falling. When she adopted a welcoming attitude toward dreams, she found she remained asleep and floated down onto a pile of soft moss in the Florida Everglades,

Happily, CMT appears to activate dream recall. The most dramatic instance I have observed occurred to a middle-aged businesswoman who swore to me that she had never remembered even one single dream fragment in her whole life. It is quite a tribute to the power of Mess Painting that during Mildred's eight weeks with CMT she reported a dream life with clear images of unconscious content that would have delighted any Freudian or Jungian analyst.

Your Dream Diary can be brief, or it can be very extensive if you have the time and enjoy recording your dreams. You can increase the amount of dream recall by writing down fragments of dreams. If you awaken late on a workday morning conscious of a long dream sequence, but need to rush through preparations to leave the house, quickly jot down some key words in the notebook you keep beside your bed. These notes may help you to recall and record more of that dream later on in the day.

Dreaming as creativity and self-healing. I believe dreams attest to our powers of imagination and creativity, and that if we look beyond the bizarre elements we often find useful messages. But at least while doing CMT, I think it is better not to assume that all dreams have great import, or to spend

Illustration 1

Illustration 2

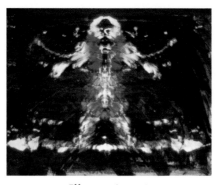

Illustration 3

Illustration 4

Illustration 5

Illustration 6

Illustration 7

Illustration 8

Illustration 9

Illustration 10

Illustration 11

On page 131 are examples of Experimental and Transcendental Paintings. Whether each is one or the other depends on your participation in viewing it and how it affects you. An important purpose of the CMT program is to free us from categorization.

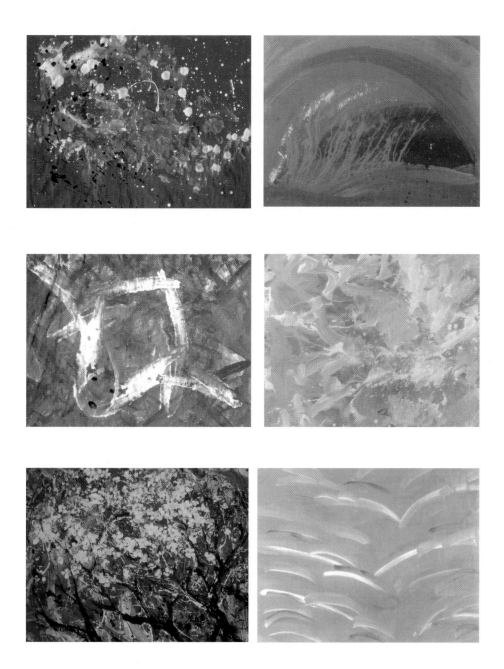

Examples of Experimental and Transcendental Paintings

Illustration 12
by Gay Luce

Yo
of
by

ney
ity
ry

turn
syste
ol e
H os cor
you c
time.

hard-
manu-
resou
materials a
ess paramet
s that allow y
dent tasks. Or
manufacturing tions in
ehensive sys

d will a ive you the
ort yo d to reach,
r produc uality
mistakes
ng this
1-800-
752-0 Ext
insights and inform hole

BASIC HINTS FOR DREAM RECALL

1. Simply deciding that you really are interested in your dreams and desire to remember them is the single most important step in dream recall.

2. Decide what means you will use to record your dreams, and prepare and place everything necessary right next to your sleeping place, so that you can use it easily — without having to get up, or even having to wake up or move around very much.

3. Focus your attention on remembering and understanding your dreams before going to sleep. These pre-sleep, "incubation" rituals can be as simple or elaborate, as specific or general as you desire.

4. If you awaken during the course of the night with a dream memory, jot down a few key words or images. Most often, this will be sufficient to stimulate a much fuller recollection of the dream upon awakening.

5. If you do not recall any dreams upon awakening, try moving into the various habitual body positions you use in sleep. Often, this simple action will trigger a dream memory.

6. If you still do not recall anything from your dreams, try imagining the faces of all the people you have the strongest emotional response to in waking life. Often one of these faces will appear in scene or setting; this is often a dream memory, and once grasped can serve to bring more of the dreams to consciousness.

7. Check your diet for B-vitamins. They appear to be important in the chemistry of dream memory for some people, and are useful in dealing with stress.

8. Consider sharing your dreams with someone you care about.... The social reinforcement of having other people with whom to share dreams most often has a significant impact upon dream recall.

- Jeremy Taylor, *Dream Work*

precious time trying to tease out some revelation. I believe the cultivation of relaxed acceptance encourages meaning to blossom when the time is ripe — for instance, when sharing the dream with a friend, or when you review your Dream Diary along with your paintings.

J. Allan Hobson's research in a sleep laboratory demonstrates that a multitude of functions are served by each of the states of sleep. His speculations relate specifically to the problem of creativity mobilization:

"During REM sleep, the brain and its mind seem to be engaging in a process of fantastic creation. It is obvious that our dreams are not simply the reliving of previous experience. On the contrary, we are often actually fabricating wholly novel ones. Thus new ideas and new feelings, and new views of old problems, can be expected to arise within dreams. These may be carried forward into the conscious mind or remain unconscious as part of our deeper creative repertoire ... the nervous system is more than a mere copying machine. While it is true that the nervous system is dependent upon external information to form its picture of the world, it also clearly uses that information to create pictures of the world against which it can test reality.

"Thus the brain of one and all is fundamentally artistic. We know this when we see the drawings of our children, but tend to discount it in our adult selves. So highly socialized are we to accept our given wake-state role that we fail to recognize the clear-cut evidence of our dreams that each of us possesses creative capability. Each of us is a surrealist at night during his or her dreams: each is a Picasso, a Dali, a Fellini — the delightful and the macabre mixed in full measure.... Dreams are truly marvelous. Why not simply enjoy them?"[1]

"Let us learn to dream, gentlemen, then perhaps we shall find the truth."

- August Kekulé

Reviewing Your Written Records

When you review your paintings at the end of each week, be sure to have your Checklist, Journal, and Dream Notebook handy. Having a written record of your emotional state and your reactions to the colors greatly enriches your appreciation and understanding of your paintings.

You will be especially glad you did your record keeping if you choose to do a final review at the end of your seven-week CMT program. Dianne discovered the value of record keeping only during her final review, when she realized what had been lost when she rebelled against the instructions to keep a Journal.

In her final review Dianne began by describing the straightforward, methodical brush strokes of her first four sessions and her struggle during each painting period with whether or not she was doing it "right." This struggle made her acutely aware of her mother's perfectionist expectations and commands (*"You can do it better!"*), and of how these demands had always made her feel diminished and inadequate.

Dianne's summary then jumped ahead to her first breakthrough, the one that convinced her she was "letting go." She explained that in her family you were expected to know exactly *why* you did something, and if you did not know or were not scrupulously searching out the reason, you were a fool, or worse, a failure. One day when it was time to write up a session, she found she couldn't write because she had almost no memory of what had been going on. Her reaction was to stop and think, *"Could it be okay to not know?"*

As she reread her Journal for her final summary, Dianne was struck by how important this particular moment had been to her. It had given her a marvelous sense of freedom. Her notes reminded her how quickly this breakthrough had changed her everyday life; soon she was able to feel quite comfortable at work when she would answer a question from those in authority with an honest *"I don't know!"*

Dianne concluded: *"During the first half of my experience with CMT I wrote a great deal in my Journal, and today when I went back over it, I was* astounded at the content. I really was amazed by connections from different sessions and different weeks .... At the halfway point when I was practicing 'not knowing and not caring,' writing in my Journal dropped down to a minimal amount. I have mixed feelings about this now. At the time it was very freeing. I had quit doing something I was 'supposed to do.' But the insights I got from the Journal earlier were so important to me that I intend to resume journal writing, and I regret that I don't have notes on a particular series of red, blue, and violet paintings. Those paintings express strong feelings but just what they were about I don't remember ....

"The process of looking at all the paintings while reading my Journal and seeing the whole flow was overwhelming. I felt weak and thought I would meditate when instead I cried and cried. I kept repeating something over and over which was related to my feelings at age four about losing my father.

"I also noticed, just before crying and crying out, a constriction in my throat which had been present the entire first week of painting and again as I began to look at the pictures today. The recollection, brought about by the words I cried out, gave me an epiphany, a core knowledge about my childhood loss from which I had been separated. I suppose that in order to survive I repressed what was too painful to endure."

CMT provided Dianne — as it does all participants — with an unparalleled opportunity to have both a visual and a verbal record of interior states. Reviewing the written material along with the paintings — combining the familiarity of expressing thoughts and feelings with pen on paper and the unfamiliar experience of Mess Painting — helps people trust the healing power of the painting process.

---

[1]J. Allan Hobson, *The Dreaming Brain,* Basic Books, 1988.

Chapter Six

The Joys and Difficulties of Mess Painting

"In the brush doing what it's doing it will stumble on what one couldn't do by oneself."
- Robert Motherwell

Your first attempts to do Mess Painting are not likely to result in anything more than a number of messy paintings. Most people find it easy to experiment and play with the materials as in Session 1. The state of consciousness associated with this exploratory mode is the familiar one that is commonly present when one is interested in learning something new. The Mess Painting experience itself is more elusive, making it harder to communicate to others or to recognize at first.

People generally have a difficult time accepting that their early messy paintings are not Mess Paintings. I had the same problem when I undertook CMT with Luthe as my guide.

I arrived in Montreal with a suitcase full of quick (less than two-minute) paintings and learned from Luthe that none of them were Mess Paintings. I was confused. If my free and easy paintings were not Mess Paintings, what should I have been doing? I became more and more bewildered as time and again Luthe dismissed my efforts. Finally he told me, "Virginia, since you came here you've just been bicycling around on the paper with your brush and paint. You are not doing Mess Painting. You haven't let go."

The next day as I started to paint I burst into tears over my failure. I was consumed with self-pity. Unlike one of my fellow students, who reacted to Luthe's disapproval with plain raw anger, I simply despaired of ever doing it right. As I wept, I painted without any interest in what was happening on the newspaper. I was unaware of what colors I was using. I did not notice that I had used black, blue, and a bit of brown on most of the paintings until late that afternoon when I emptied my drying racks and stacked my paintings for the night's review. Still the significance of this fact eluded me until Luthe gave me positive feedback on this session.

At our nightly meetings I had repeatedly asked Luthe, "Is this one a Mess Painting? Is this one?" He had patiently explained that we were not to be particularly interested in any individual painting. On the contrary what we should be looking for during the review was spontaneous natural repetition.

His directive did not mean much to me until after the session in which I had tearfully broken through my barrier to letting go. In the group meeting that night Luthe had me spread all my paintings on the floor, and pointed out that almost all of them had the same colors. It was readily apparent to everyone in the room that there were seven sequential "look-alike" paintings in which not only were the proportions of blue, black, and brown more or less the same, but the brush work was also very similar. Moreover, these paintings seemed to reflect my despair.

This visual display did more for me than words. Now I understood what was meant by spontaneous natural repetition. I could see the rhythm of the brush work and the color relationships repeating in the series, and how the other paintings in the session differed. I knew that I had not given conscious attention to creating a series in which each looked like a continuation of the previous one. It surprised me that just looking at them evoked some of the pain I had felt earlier in the day.

Later, in guiding my clients into the Mess Painting experience, I began to use the metaphor of a family to describe what would begin to appear in their paintings as they let go. People are surprised to see their emotions reflected in their paintings, and to realize that the number of members in a Mess Painting family depends on the length of time a particular emotional state persists, or is allowed to continue without being artificially interrupted. Sometimes in a longer-than-usual session two series will appear — two separate families of paintings, each family employing its own emotional expression.

The only way to enter into spontaneous painting is to get out from under the control of your logical mind and into what Luthe called a "no-thought" mode. Mess Painting, as one client put it, is a marvelous vehicle for "cutting loose." There is no use trying to think, to analyze, to judge your way into Mess Painting. You need to trust that your arm/hand/brush will, as the above quote by Motherwell suggests, *stumble on what one couldn't do by oneself.*"

When you let go, the painting situation becomes similar to meditation, where a thought is allowed to flow into, through, and out of consciousness without disturbing the meditation. To get to this point in Mess Painting, you may need to deal harshly with the habit of thoughtfully, actively responding to what you see. You may need to attack an area that looks lovely and deliberately, forcefully, totally wipe it out!

Eventually you will fall into a very rhythmical repetition of brush strokes. Rhythm provides direct access to the unconscious, and so will help you move closer to the deeper purpose of CMT. This purpose is to help you to connect more deeply with your essential and authentic self, to its inner wisdom, and to its linkage with the universe, the divine, whatever your name for the ineffable may be.

If reaching that state requires clearing out psychological garbage by revisiting present trauma and/or old history, Mess Painting provides an environment where that can happen. If you can stay with the seemingly meaningless nature of Mess Painting long enough, you will accumulate new perceptions to help you live your life with more harmony, have greater clarity in decision making, and move forward with desired behavioral changes.

Artist and teacher Peter London, in his book *No More Secondhand Art*, makes many observations about the creative process that are pertinent to this non-thinking aspect of Mess Painting:

"We know we are addressing the resources of the subconscious mind when we begin to make things (sounds, images, gestures) without knowing what we are doing or what it may mean. The uninitiated dismiss this activity as meaningless — and unfortunately, they are in part correct, it is meaningless. But they fail to understand that this is a necessary phase of a much more elaborate series of mental operations that do eventuate in meaning. Misapprehending the activity as a complete act, they never proceed along to the next phases and accordingly never gain, indeed never could gain, the rewards....

"The creative process is, to a significant degree, a somatic act, one in which the physical body expresses what is known in those portions of the brain that operate nonverbally and that rely upon image and gesture to convey their knowledge."

An appreciation of the importance of natural repetition comes only through experience. If you have been involved with meditation, prayer, or breathwork, you already know that regular, time-after-time practice is essential.

In CMT you are told to begin painting with a relaxed arm and to move it at an easy pace — with fingers, hand and wrist following what the arm wishes to do, and allowing the brush to dance across the paper beyond the edge onto the work surface — while freely vocalizing with nonsense or animal sounds, humming, singing, or whatever. The act of painting is to proceed as effortlessly as possible, with the whole body relaxed and with a mental attitude of letting go.

In my first days in Montreal with Luthe, instead of relaxing my body and vocalizing I was silent as I painted. But my mind was a beehive of self-talk: *"How can I guide others through this process if I can't do it myself? What a financial disaster this trip is going to be!"* It is reasonable to want to succeed and to have something to show for the time and money invested, but such concerns block letting go.

I did follow some of the instructions. My brush strokes crossed over each other. My color selection was random. The paintings were messy. However, certain technical errors stood out. My brush strokes rarely went beyond the margins of the paper onto the working surface. The application of the paint had a tentative appearance. This, coupled with the clues provided by my Checklists — the absence of vocalization or body movements, the tension I felt during and after painting — indicated a failure to let go, and hence the presence of self-sabotage.

Examples of Paintings

Often my clients, frustrated at the ambiguity of some of the instructions for Mess Paintings, ask to see an example. My answer has always been that it is not in their best interest to look at someone else's Mess Paintings. Creating paintings that look like the messy paintings of others is pointless. The task everyone faces is to let go. Once that happens, each person's style or styles of doing spontaneous, repetitive paintings will evolve quite naturally. Think how long and how much repetition it takes to become a tennis player. Becoming comfortable with doing Mess Painting is quick compared with the time it takes to learn a sport. Have patience with yourself, and respect your own rate of learning to let go.

My reasons for not providing examples of Mess Paintings have sometimes fallen on unreceptive ears, and some people have made my refusal a reason to quit. But by dealing with the frustrations inherent in CMT as they arise, each participant eventually creates Mess Paintings that are truly his or her own.

In this book I have broken with my established precedent and provided glimpses of Mess Paintings (See Illustrations on pages 133-136). The illustrations are not whole Mess Paintings, but sections of the paintings shown in their actual size. From these color illustrations you will be able to appreciate the rhythmic, overlapping brush strokes and the use of color, without being influenced by the overall appearance of a complete painting.

Importance of Observing the Rules

Self-sabotage can take many forms. People sometimes change the rules because they do not understand their purpose. Looking for ways to improve on the instructions is extremely counterproductive. It might appear that the rules for Mess Painting are obsessively precise. But it is the framework created by these carefully thought-out rules that provides a safe place for experiencing freedom.

One common example of rule-breaking is playing music while painting. Music is a powerful tool to alter emotion, but in CMT the goal is to have the stimulus arise from within.

DO'S AND DON'TS OF MESS PAINTING

DO:

- *Use one brush for each color of paint, and alternate colors with each brushful.*

- *Cover at least 75 percent of a double-page newspaper surface in almost two minutes by painting the biggest mess possible.*

- *Aim at producing about 15 to 20 no-thought Mess Paintings in one session.*

- *Engage in one painting session on at least four different days of the week.*

- *Continue with regular painting sessions (four times a week) for at least six to eight weeks.*

(Continued)

DO NOT COMMIT THESE TECHNICAL ERRORS:

- *Avoidance of going over the paper margin.*

- *Intentional direction and interruption of brush strokes (e.g., straight, horizontal, vertical lines, circles, squares, wave patterns, series of dots, zigzags, spirals).*

- *Aesthetic, rationalistic considerations (e.g., in choice and application of colors, composition).*

- *Desire to impress others and concern about being ridiculed.*

- *Concern about splashing paint, dirty fingers and clothes.*

- *Inadequate preparations (e.g., lack of paint, numbered newspapers, space for drying, unstable sliding paper, improper location of paint, inadequate protection of room).*

- *Preoccupation with ardent wishes for "creative inspirations," "illuminating insights," or "impressive changes."*

- *Overzealous production of impressive numbers of paintings; overconcern with time-keeping (e.g., racing against time).*

- *Improper duration of painting sessions (e.g., painting to exhaustion, forcing oneself to reach a certain number, to finish newspaper supply, etc.)*

- *Using brushes in both hands, or more than one brush at a time.*

- *Self-designed "improvements" on the instructions.*

- *Closing eyes while painting.*

- *Distractions such as radio, music, restless pets, curious family members.*

- *Inadequate release of expression through crying, laughing, aggression, singing, grunting, swearing, talking, motor discharges.*

- Adapted from Wolfgang Luthe,
The Creativity Mobilization Technique

Most people, even when they are supposedly Mess Painting, make one aesthetic choice of color after another. Then, aware that this is a "no-no," some begin to paint with their eyes closed to solve the problem. This is an unproductive maneuver, since the exposure of eye and brain to the brilliant colors while Mess Painting stimulates emotion and memory.

Barbara, a serious, hard-working young woman with two jobs, one in publishing and one in art therapy, had other strategies for bending the rules. At first she could not refrain from fussing with the brushes to keep the colors clean and pure. As soon as a brush got dirty she would throw it into her bucket of water and reach for a clean brush to replace it. She had purchased many extra brushes for this purpose.

Barbara happily offered her improvement on the CMT instructions to others in her group who had expressed dismay at seeing their paint get dirty. I told her that this tactic reflected an attitude that would prevent her from letting go into spontaneous painting, but she persisted in trying to have her own way. She bought a large thick sponge, which she kept to one side of her painting, and would wipe the dirty brush across it before putting it back into its pot. Barbara discovered on her own that this, too, was not in her best interest, and was honest enough to report her mistake to the group. She finally was able to accept that her concern over how the colors looked was preventing her from being in the state of passive concentration and passive acceptance necessary for Mess Painting.

Others decide to use a brush in each hand — or two brushes in one hand — which produces messiness but interferes with spontaneous repetition. Annie employed this stratagem, as well as many other errors, during her the first few weeks of painting:

"I'm having a serious problem with all this structure and I'm fighting it. My family was great on rules and I hated them. Generally I just ignore structure, and here I'm accepting it or trying to. It's been a hellacious week. One day I did two very short sessions because I was interrupted by my neighbor who was having someone cut down my hedge. Today I found all my paint pots with dried-out

paint — I hadn't read the part in the instructions about covering the paint till this morning. I tried dealing with all these chunks of dried-up paint but that didn't work. When I did get the paint fixed up and got started again, I thought the colors sucked, I couldn't connect with any of them — may just have been holding off my feelings. I didn't connect with the painting at all, it was like I was doing a job. I felt stupid, that was a big pervasive quality of the whole session.

"I'm trying to follow the directions but I find myself painting with two hands. I hate one-handed paintings and dragging one brush across the paper. And blobs of brown in the white make me puke. I can see if I'm going to enjoy this process I'll have to embrace the structure with a little more grace. Maybe I should move inside; I don't have any privacy outside where I paint; there are often people walking by."

Annie finally realized she was not having any of the experiences and benefits that other members of her group were getting. Admitting to herself that she had wasted several weeks fighting the instructions, she finally moved her work table inside and began to follow the directions, much as it went against the grain at first. She began to correct the many errors she had been making — numbering only the sheets of newspaper she expected to be using that day; not stacking the drying trays but instead starting with the newspaper on a wet drying tray and after painting, laying the trays down somewhere in the yard (after they were dry, getting her paintings in numerical order for evaluation purposes was a difficult and time-consuming task). Annie rearranged her work schedule so that it couldn't cut into her time for Mess Painting as it had in the past. She was still unwilling to plan enough time for both painting and the necessary reflection and relaxation afterwards. By the end of seven weeks she was barely into Mess Painting, but acknowledged that what she had learned from confronting her self-destructive patterns was worth all the trouble and frustration.

A common problem among beginning painters is ending the session too soon. Some of my clients have claimed that they did this because they were worried about the paintings having enough time to dry before the weekly meeting. I view this as self-sabotage because the painter has not made the necessary provisions in the painting space — a fan or electric heater, an open window for air circulation — to ensure that the paintings will dry in time.

Feeling tired, bored, or frustrated after a session suggests that something that began to happen during the session was interrupted. It is not a trivial matter to stop too soon. Some hours later you may experience symptoms such as moodiness, unexplainable fatigue, irritability, anxiety, malaise, mild nausea, headache, or even an asthma attack, as did my client Maria, quoted later in this chapter. Such complaints may stem from other causes, such as sleep deprivation; but just as an adequate painting session can engender extremely positive feelings, a poorly handled session can have a negative aftermath.

After a session in his second week of CMT, Bruce was left with a feeling of depression. He realized this was due to his failure to go further into his sadness while painting:

"I began the session feeling down. While painting I felt sadness, a lump in my throat, wanting to cry but couldn't, lonely. Then I got into a series with many mostly black, followed by a couple of attempts to lighten up, then a couple more dark ones, then I switched to yellow. So I ended up with a light, a dark, a light — I didn't want to stay in the dark. And after the session I still felt down, lonely."

When negative emotions are present it is essential that there be no interruption of the painting process, even if it means doing thirty or more paintings, until the emotion subsides by itself. A newcomer to CMT may not understand that such errors as interrupting the use of dark colors that accompany painful material with consciously chosen lighter and brighter colors, or stopping too soon, or needing to cry but resisting, may result in headaches, depression, or disturbing dreams.

A common technical error is not getting enough paint onto the newspaper, either because the paint is too thin, or because not enough time is spent on the painting. When paint is too thin you can't see the brush strokes and whether they repeat. My client Helen made both these errors. A group member pointed out that she was not getting enough paint on the paper, commenting that the paintings all looked as if they had been done in thirty seconds. Helen's response was: "I really needed to see the color" — meaning that she didn't want to put so much paint on that the colors would become muddy. When the same problem was pointed out at the next session, Helen replied: "I was restraining myself so the paintings would dry in time." Helen always had a good reason why the paint was skimpy or too thin, and for a long time this prevented her from entering into Mess Painting.

Helen's excuses are good examples of self-sabotage. Luthe told me that the worst instance he had experienced was a client who placed the newspaper on the drying tray, poured several colors of paint on the paper, lifted the tray in the air, and spun and moved it around so that the colors ran into and over each other. The client did a whole session this way, and then brought it to Luthe for evaluation. Luthe dismissed him.

I do not take offense at such blatant disregard of instructions. Rather I explain to my clients that erroneous methods will prevent them from finding their own organic patterns of repetition, and thus their own unique Mess Painting experience.

A number of activities that might seem helpful for getting into creating Mess Paintings are in fact *barriers* to doing so. Looking for "insight" and for something fantastic to happen, or forcing yourself to produce a large number of paintings in order to "make progress," are not useful. In fact they will certainly interfere with your ability to move into spontaneous painting.

Breaking Through Resistance

Many people go through a period of resistance where they do many fewer than the necessary four sessions per week. The lethargy and boredom experienced at this time is not unusual; I have observed that it commonly takes place during the fourth week.

Perhaps the practical, analytical, logical, rational, product- and time-oriented part of us becomes impatient at this point with its loss of dominance, and needs to be fed relevant intellectual fare to drum up some confidence in this odd undertaking. I therefore provide my clients with an annotated book list and a collection of readings. I do not expect them to read everything, but pursuing the material they are attracted to seems to encourage them to continue working when they hit a patch of resistance. These readings, and other relevant material, are listed in the Annotated Bibliography at the end of this book.

In his little gem of a book, *Zen and the Art of Archery*, Eugene Herrigal describes the extreme difficulty he had in a situation requiring much the same attitudes as Mess Painting — learning archery in the Zen manner. This required a letting go (of the arrow), with a total lack of concern about the outcome (hitting the bull's eye). What Herrigal's Zen archery Master had to say to him on the subject of letting go should also be of interest to the Mess Painter:

"You must hold the drawn bowstring like a little child holding the proffered finger. It grips it so firmly that one marvels at the strength of the tiny fist. And when it lets the finger go, there is not the lightest jerk. Do you know why? Because a child doesn't think: I will let go of the finger in order to grasp this other thing. Completely unself-consciously, without purpose, the child turns from one to the other....

"The right shot at the right moment does not come, because you do not let go of yourself. You do not wait for fulfillment, but brace yourself for failure... You cannot wait without purpose.... You continually ask yourself: 'Shall I be able to manage it?'... You call forth something yourself that ought to happen independently of you."

Getting out of one's own way is not easy. Schoolteacher Lisa's summary of her CMT experience during a summer vacation shows how difficult it can be:

"In the first few weeks, any day that I had scheduled myself to paint I procrastinated all day long. The more hours that went by, the more depressed I felt. My throat tightened and sometimes I became hoarse. Even though I had chosen to do CMT, I interpreted it as WORK to be done. After I finally did paint,

I would feel very tired — resisting takes a lot of energy.

"Being playful was impossible for me. The first moment of spattering was pleasurable but immediately I felt self-conscious, and wondered whether I was doing the spattering right. I hesitated before each and every brush stroke, and I doubt I ever covered more than sixty percent of any newspaper in those first three weeks.

"One day I said to myself: 'Why am I doing this when it makes me so miserable? I've a notion to call Virginia and terminate my commitment. After all, there is some wisdom in knowing where you are and in honoring your feelings. On the other hand, I'm not one to quit what I start.' And I didn't quit.

"Then in the fourth week, after mowing the lawn on a warm, moist summer evening, I went into my painting shed and suddenly as I painted I cried and cried about the time I came home from school and couldn't find my rag doll — a doll I slept with every night. My grandmother and my mother had sat me down and informed me that they had decided I was too old to sleep with it and that the doll was too worn out to keep. They had sent it away with the trash pickup.

"My grief while painting turned into rage as I remembered how they, including my father, had pretended my beloved old tabby cat had run away when in fact it had been 'put down.' Never with my family did I feel free enough to truly express anger directly toward my parents and grandmother. It was too threatening for me as a child and too threatening for them. If they could not accept their own anger, how could they accept mine?

"As I was expressing my fury that night, spattering became a catalyst. It gave me permission to feel the anger, to pound the paper with the brushes, to swear, to release the raw emotions and to let go of them.

"In the next two weeks I painted my way through some more emotional sessions, as well as bland boring ones where my old resistances — self-criticism, judging the process ridiculous, etc. — reappeared until finally in the very last week I had the pleasure of two dreamy sessions full of light colors and pleasant fantasies. And then my summer vacation was over."

Expressing Feelings

Eleanor had no difficulty at all in getting right into Mess Painting because of what happened to her just before she was about to start her first session. Eleanor had set up her painting area over the weekend. On Monday she came home from a day full of problems at her job as a social worker, with the plan to paint that evening. She found her apartment door wide open and her TV, radio, tape recorder, and cassette player gone. The whole place had been trashed, and many belongings broken. She had no insurance, and could not easily afford to replace the stolen and damaged furnishings.

After dealing with police, landlord, and locksmith, Eleanor began to paint. There was no hesitation in selecting the colors that spoke to her anger and frustration. Without thought she immediately grabbed for red, black, and brown and used them exclusively for much of the session. Someone else in a similar situation might have chosen red, black, and violet, or brown and red. I had one client who found that only black interspersed with yellow felt right when expressing her rage.

As Eleanor painted, she hit the paper with her brushes and often tore it. Being physically aggressive in addition to swearing, spitting, and yelling released her rage at the thieves and their violation of her territory in a profoundly satisfying way. At about painting number seventeen, her colors changed to brown and violet, and tears erupted over the recent death of a dear friend in an accident. She wept through the rest of the session, and when all her drying trays were full did another six paintings, placing them on the floor. Then, exhausted, she fell into bed.

The next evening Eleanor caught up with her record keeping, and more tears accompanied her writing about the previous night's session. She almost convinced herself that she shouldn't paint again until she was more rested and had finished cleaning up after the thieves. But something urged her back into her painting space in the guest bedroom.

In this second session, again using brown and violet, Eleanor continued to weep over the loss of her friend — all the tears she had not been able to shed during the month since the fatal accident. Toward the end of the session she began to feel calmer, and was able to use other colors. Expressing her rage had dissolved the barriers to weeping — barriers that years of early parental training had imposed.

Because of the turmoil with which she had entered into Mess Painting, Eleanor waited until the second week to explore time-sense training and the exploratory mode of playing with the materials. In the following weeks it was comparatively easy for her to let go into Mess Painting, and while no other single session was as dramatic as her first, there were others that she felt were of equal value. Mess Painting helped Eleanor clarify several important issues, including coming to a decision to move to a city where she could live in a CoHousing Community where she would own her own private, completely equipped, tiny town house, but be with her neighbors in the commonly-owned recreation building for cooperatively prepared dinners and for socializing afterwards.[1] No longer alienated from her deepest feelings, she was increasingly free to use her energy for living her life as fully and happily as possible.

Like Eleanor, you may be someone for whom the expression of emotion is difficult. If even the privacy of your painting sessions doesn't help you to let go into the expression of feelings, or the crying that needs to be done, I recommend you try the Autogenic "Crying" Exercise on page 157. This can be very helpful for getting away from your logical mind and into your emotions.

Beginning attempts at Mess Painting often go back and forth between dark and light paintings. One client asked: "If you are feeling bad and grab for yellow, should you stop yourself?" The answer is yes — unless for you yellow is a color that matches dark, heavy feelings. Avoiding bad feelings and trying to move to a more neutral state is pointless. Alone in your work space, when unpleasant emotions come up it is best to get into them instead of comforting yourself with colors you especially like. You can always use painting as a way to feel better; but to use painting as a catharsis you need to have the courage to go deeper — to accept what is happening and stick with it.

Beth, a young artist and graduate student in art therapy, was quite pleased that CMT gave her access to buried feelings: *"It has been very rare in my life that I can get really angry. Really deeply, honestly in touch with that younger hurt scared part of myself that holds so much. CMT is one of the only processes I have learned where I can truly reach and access that buried part of me. It is one of the only times I can remember when I could totally express my emotions and feel what on other occasions I would suppress. CMT is a safe, expansive tool that took me to anger, rage, sadness, and joy as they are meant to be experienced."*

Beth also noted: *"When I felt sulky and angry, it felt good to slash and punch strokes at the paper. The feeling of anger could evoke that method of painting — or vice versa."* When you suspect that there are feelings lurking in the wings that you are not getting to, you can try painting in a manner which would express them and see if this will bring out the feelings.

Autogenic Exercises for Letting Go

Fortunately, the kind of letting go necessary for the CMT experience can be deliberately encouraged; there are things you can do to help yourself move on into true Mess Painting. The following exercises are part the standard repertoire of Autogenic Training and Therapy. I teach them to people who have inhibitions about allowing sounds to come out while Mess Painting. If you have been inhibited about vocalizing while painting, these exercises may help you remove your blocks to letting go. Practice them during private time alone, at home or in a car. You may need to run a vacuum cleaner or keep the car motor idling to avoid feeling silly or worrying about being overheard.

The Crying Exercise. Dr. David A. Goodman noted that *"Weeping may hold the key to mental health. Primal tears are the key to understanding the phenomenon. Tears of grief, loneliness and loss are the solution that dissolves the walls of the unconscious and that dissipates encapsulated pain."*[2]

Dr. William Frey, biochemist at St. Paul University of Minnesota Biochemistry Department, has studied the chemistry of tears and has found that they contain high concentrations of stress hormones. These hormones do not occur in tears resulting from irritants such as onions. Clearly, if there is a release of stress hormones with tears, then the blocking of that release may result in the buildup of stress hormones. Crying is an important biologic function, and the shedding of tears is *central* — not incidental — to the resolution of neurosis. Tears, Frey found, not only remove toxic substances from the eye, they also have a precise role in the removal of toxic biochemical substances from the entire system.[3]

CRYING EXERCISE

To do the crying exercise, find a comfortable place to sit, where you will have complete privacy. Begin by thinking of something sad — even if you don't feel sad, make sounds as though you were. As you pretend to cry it is not necessary to produce real tears, but if tears come they are to be welcomed and allowed to flow until they stop naturally.

Do not force tears by cutting up a raw onion. Instead, concentrate on producing the kind of rapid, gasping breathing and the sounds that are present in a good cry. Remember the variety of body movements that go along with intense grief.

What would your shoulder girdle do? Would your chest heave? If you were in a play, what would you be doing with your body and facial expressions to show grief? Another possibility in pretending to cry is to experiment with the distinctions between sounding like, for example, a hurt, a sad, and a lonely two-year-old, or like someone whose child has died.

Occasionally Mess Painting will open the floodgates to all the tears that should have been cried in the past. If that happens for you, you may weep through many consecutive painting sessions. If you find this disturbing, please trust that the vast intelligence of your inner healer knows how much crying you need to do.

The need to cry during a painting session may have little or nothing to do with the current situation. Sometimes copious tears are associated with a need to discharge aggression. Many people have been taught in childhood to block crying and continue to do so throughout their lives. Consequently this kind of tension release is not easily available to them. We all know the wonderful sense of relief that a good cry can bring, especially when there has been no holding back. Interfering, instead of allowing tears to subside naturally, is truly ill-advised, especially if the crying is part of an immediate sorrow. If the necessary tears are held back in such a situation, the acute tension of grief and loss may simply turn into a more tolerable pattern of fear and anxiety. Repeated and prolonged sobbing without an immediate cause may seem strange, but it is quite normal for past grief to reappear, especially if it was insufficiently dealt with at the time.

Mess Painting offers an opportunity for expressing grief that has not been adequately dealt with before. Too often when there is a death in the family, one member takes charge, and by repressing his or her grief is able to take care of everyone else. When Mess Painting opens the floodgates, such individuals may become anxious that their weeping will never stop.

This was the experience of a middle-aged social worker who always stepped in and took care of everyone and everything whenever there was a death of a relative or friend. She wept steadily through the first eighteen of her twenty-five painting sessions. During the first four weeks she needed a lot of reassurance that her sobbing while painting was a necessary and positive response which would stop by itself when she had cried enough. And it did.

In the mythology of many cultures, the very creation of our world comes directly from crying. One such myth is from the Algonquin Indians: *"In the beginning there was nothing but water. On the water was a boat and in the boat was a man who cried because he had no idea what his fate would be.... And the Moshush rat came from the water and said, 'Grandfather, why are you crying?' And then she fished up the earth for him."*[4]

Sue, a young psychotherapist, found in Mess Painting the key for completing the memory of a two-week stay in an orphanage when she was about three years old. In various kinds of therapy, Jungian, Reichian, and Gestalt, she had at times focused on her awareness that something dreadful had happened to her in the orphanage — something that included being swung up in the air by a woman caretaker she had hated — but she could never recall anything more.

Naturally this subject came up while painting, and as she thought about the woman, her anger grew and she screamed curses as she made numerous quick paintings with slashes and blotches of brown and black paint. She was working in a rented space, the basement of a Korean Church, and was making so much noise that the minister couldn't resist unlocking the door and asking if she was all right. She assured him that she was, and was able to return to Mess Painting in spite of the interruption. At the end of the session she did a crude, childlike portrait of the horrible witch caretaker (See Illustration 2, page 129). But whatever had happened between them remained a mystery — until the following day.

In the next session, after she had wet the work surface and was smoothing out the newspaper her eyes were drawn to an ad with an illustration of a syringe. It was an ordinary kind available for purchase in drugstores, about six inches long with a rubber bulb and a plastic nozzle.

When she saw the ad she remembered that at age 14, when standing beside her boyfriend as he opened his tool chest, she had been horrified at the sight of such a syringe and angrily had asked, "Why do you have that?" He had seemed bewildered by her outburst and had replied, "Well, uh, I use it for oiling motors." Remembering that encounter brought more angry feelings, and Sue slashed away at the newspaper with blacks, reds, and browns, shouting and cursing.

Suddenly she was back in the orphanage and the caretaker was brutally giving her an enema. She was struggling wildly. The nozzle, the water hurt. She screamed and cried. As the child must have done so long ago, Sue wept now for having been so violated. She went on painting furiously, with tears flowing, until her rage and sobbing stopped of itself.

The Verbal Garbage Exercise. This exercise, which does not require the complete privacy that the crying one does, is less demanding and is a fine way to lighten up before beginning to paint.

VERBAL GARBAGE EXERCISE

While getting ready to paint, play with all sorts of animal noises — grunts, barks, meows, moos, snorts, or babble — "Da da daa di doo doo oo fut foot boot goot," etc. Making these sounds is a way to remind yourself that this is your private time for total freedom.

A young professional artist who had been practicing in this way commented: *"One day as I was painting, feeling irritable, I began without thought to make animal noises, snarling and snapping as I worked. My strokes, my gestures with the brushes, began to come out of these noises, and I found I was working from my feelings in a way that I had not done before."*

Unusual Sensations While Painting

It is important to be patient with your own individual patterns of reactivity at certain stages of Mess Painting. Suppression of crying or insufficient unloading of aggression tend to amplify anxiety. Brain-disturbing material may cause sensory discharges such as feelings of dizziness, numbness, itching, and/or distortion of the body image.

My client Bruce marked a 4 on his Checklist for "change in body image" after a session that included a series of mostly pink paintings: *"I felt ridiculous doing pink, but tried to let it go where it led. As I continued and got into the pink series in the Mess Painting mode, I felt the change in body image — I felt expanded a bit, like I took up more space."*

Unusual sensations may seem unwelcome, surprising or bizarre to the painter. It is best to allow them to work themselves out through the painting sessions; they tend to disappear when correctly supported by passive acceptance.

Usually the physical manifestations are not so extreme. Many people, for example, get mild electric-like tingling while Mess Painting, but only rarely does it approach the Kundalini-like experience of Bob, a shy man in his fifties:

"During the second week, I noted a metallic taste in my mouth which was associated with a feeling of calm well-being, of passive concentration, of being lost in the present. Tensions eased, and stressors decreased in their negative effect. In a later session (on the 231st painting), I felt the familiar metallic taste in my mouth and then experienced an electric charge throughout my body. It concentrated in my painting arm which seemed to be guided by an unseen force, and then it went to my spinal cord like a bolt of lighting which shot up to my head and beyond. I felt BEYOND my body, as if there were a second layer to my being, and I had to laugh and exclaim aloud because I was overflowing with joy. It was a spiritual feeling that defies words. The feeling was euphoric, ecstatic, and powerful in the sense of invulnerability. I even felt it in my eyebrows.

"CMT is the beginning for me, a commencement. For the first time in my life I am calm and self-assured. Later, in addition to gleaning knowledge about what I didn't want to do, I became aware of the myriad projects that I do want to undertake."

For Beth, the unusual occurrences manifested in the paintings themselves as well as in her body:

"Shapes started appearing about halfway through the course and continued till the end that were really amazing. I still have no idea what to make of them. Around the fourth week or so this ominous shape appeared out of the right side of

the pages. Being left-handed, the fact that it mostly came from the right side seemed really interesting to me. It seemed that about halfway through many sessions this thing would appear and grow and come alive from the page. Then at some point it would be gone and once again the pages of newspaper would be completely covered in tempera paint. At times the Mess Painting was reminiscent of the act, the reliving of the abuse my body and heart withstood during earlier days as a teenager. At times while Mess Painting, I could actually feel the act finally over and I would make small quiet repetitive strokes on the page, as if comforting a small child. Over and over I would just stand kind of 'spaced out' and detached, stroking the page with the paintbrush in small, quiet movements. It was quite a contrast to the aggressive hard fast movements that had preceded these moments of my sessions."

Everyone comes to CMT with a different life story and with different things that need attending to. Jack, an environmental lawyer in his early forties with a wry, quick wit, was still coping with the death of his mother, father, and twin sister in an airplane crash eighteen years earlier. He felt that because this tragedy had not been adequately handled at the time, uncomfortable distances had developed between himself, his brother, and his remaining sister. This troubled him greatly. During the weeks of CMT he thought a lot about really reaching out to his sister, and before the seven weeks were over he acted on this decision.

In his summary Jack, who has always been quite ambidextrous, wrote: "When I started, I was not sure which hand to paint with. After some experimentation, I found that the use of my left hand invoked more of an emotional connection to what I was painting, with less intellectual analysis and head talk. But for some time I had difficulty when I moved my left arm/hand across the center of my body and over to the right side of the newspaper. Every time my arm and brush did this, I would feel dizzy, disoriented, and sometimes nauseated. After the second week (eight painting sessions later) those feelings went away and I was freer in my brush strokes.

"One session during the fourth week I started out very de-energized — I had

had a lot of difficulties in my work day. I absent-mindedly started with my right hand, and when I realized this I went ahead and painted the whole session that way. By far the worst session I had. Painting with my right hand made me dizzy, nauseated, gave me a headache. I was cursing Virginia, I couldn't wait to get finished. I was really surprised to find how difficult, or different, it was with my right hand. And again I had trouble moving my arm across the plane of my body, this time to the left.

"The next session, I went back to left-handed painting. I felt a lot of freedom; painting was completely secondary and I really didn't give it much thought most of the session. Time passed very quickly, singing, animal noises. Lots of surprise — I'd be painting but not paying attention and then would wonder how the painting got there — I would feel like I could walk out of the room and still be in there painting at the same time — no connection at all to the painting except that I'm enjoying watching it."

Watching the painting form itself as he was painting it created such a non-ordinary state of consciousness that Jack found it hard to put into words:

"There were a number of paintings with a dragon, represented by the black — these were forces, not evil or even bad, but the things you have to overcome.... The dragons are, like a challenge, not bad but with repercussions — if you're defeated you're dead — not frightening but serious. Blue and purple was like humanity coming into the struggle.... When I interjected myself into the drama I picked violet and blue.

"It was all about struggle, but not negative struggle — it felt good to do this and get it out. The next session, as I painted and the dragon came out, there was more interaction between colors, I was singing 'Knights in White Satin,' interested in seeing where the paints hit the newspaper and where they would go, the interplay between things... The black is the abyss, behind the dragon is the abyss. I had no fear so it was not a negative abyss but the unknown, in the middle of the painting like a giant hole I was filling in. Fighting the dragon became more of a dance. Dance the dance. The dance of life and death, the dance of being and non-being.

"The next session I started out feeling good, lots of energy.... Painting that day seemed angelic, not struggle related though that had not been negative. It was reverence and revelatory, joy and beauty, no active struggle. When painting becomes meditative, the universe opens up at the stroke of a brush."

Jack's experiences are a good example of the out-of-the-ordinary states of consciousness that sometimes occur during Mess Painting. They are to be accepted as normal, and require no analysis or interpretation. The inner healer is working something out non-verbally. It should be given respect, and the time to do whatever it needs to do. Acceptance of these odd sensations will free up energy for creative action.

Facilitating Self-Healing

We can all be grateful that a cut finger repairs itself easily unless further trauma interferes, such as rubbing dirt into the wound. This innate capacity of our whole being — body/mind/spirit — to repair damage suggests that we are programmed, when provided with a supportive, health-promoting environment, to facilitate self-healing. But when the body/mind/spirit is overloaded with past and present emotional and physical pain and abuse, then the energy that our inner healer could bring to maintaining good health and furthering creativity is expended in simply holding things together.

Our inner healer seems to recognize in Mess Painting an environment that is helpful for neutralizing trauma, and it is also capable of responding negatively if that opportunity vanishes. Hence just as a full, uninhibited Mess Painting session brings positive results, undesirable consequences have been observed again and again when Mess Painting sessions were ended prematurely or when emerging feelings were avoided.

The instructions for Mess Painting have been carefully thought out and clinically tested, and should be taken seriously. Otherwise, unexpected and often unpleasant symptoms may occur. The following account is a good example of the folly of ignoring even part of the directions.

Maria was a beautiful Mediterranean-looking woman with a very expressive voice, who gave a lot of attention to her appearance. She and her therapist were aware that they were at an impasse because of Maria's inability to get in touch with her feelings. They had both read an article of mine on CMT, and decided that doing Mess Painting might help solve the problem.

Maria followed my instructions for the brush work. She allowed her brush to move freely over the paper and to go beyond the margins onto the work surface, and her paintings were appropriately repetitious from one to the next. But the colors she used were always light and in lovely combinations. She reported at the group meetings that she remained completely silent while enjoying this rhythmical way of painting.

As she persisted in avoiding the dark colors, she became aware of the contrast between the beautiful pastel colors she consciously created by using a lot of white, and the shame she carried inside herself. The way she was painting was the way she had always behaved — never revealing to anyone the abuse she had suffered as a child or the macho behavior she endured now from a husband who saw to his own needs with little consideration of hers. Instead she always spoke well of her life. As part of the image she cultivated, she was always beautifully groomed, and throughout her twenty-five years of married life she had obsessively vacuumed the whole house every day.

Her color-controlled, silent painting style continued for many sessions, and then asthma, which she had not had since childhood, suddenly appeared. It lasted two weeks, not leaving until she had completely let go. Maria wrote of this important experience in her final summary:

"Once I broke the silence and gave up making pretty pictures, my paintings became very dark like the shame that I carried for my parents that I had never been able to expose to others or to myself. Finally I was able to express anger during many sessions. I cursed loudly. I slammed gobs of paint on the paper and also tore it because of the pressure I put on the brush. And while wadding up the ugly black paintings with the paint oozing through my fingers, I felt the intense anger and hatred I had and still have for all those who have abused me.

"In subsequent sessions I felt grief, sadness and loneliness just as I had felt

them as a child when I couldn't talk to anyone, when I had to be silent and pretend not to have any needs. My sobs and tears came from a very deep and wounded place."

Maria's experience supports Luthe's conviction that the brain readily recognizes an opportunity for unloading, and sees to it that unpleasant symptoms will ensue if the person stops painting too soon or suppresses the anger or grief that is ready to surface. Such behavior prevents the neutralization of troubling material from both the recent and the remote past. It seems that the brain, like other organs of the body, wants to move toward wholeness and welcomes assistance in doing so.

During the last three weeks of her CMT experience, Maria began to behave differently in the group meetings. When one of her paintings triggered an emotional response, she stayed with it. She was willing to let the other women see her cry or become angry instead of quickly turning the painting over, suppressing her emotion, and going on to showing the next one. She also discovered that her desire to change her behavior with friends and family was strengthened by speaking honestly in the group. Her paintings again became full of lovely colors, but this time they reflected her growing self-confidence. In her daily existence Maria was exploring her new freedom — freedom from the shoulds, the shalt nots, and the must dos that had governed her behavior all her life.

After completing CMT the first time, Maria returned to her therapist to work on issues concerning her adult children. A few months later, she joined another Mess Painting group. This time her summary of the experience was simply a list of the changes she had made during the second CMT period:

"I stopped using the vacuum cleaner and hired someone to come one-half day a week. I find I am unconcerned when on occasion that person doesn't show up. I thumb my nose at the telephone answering machine and check for messages only once a day. I choose when to answer the calls. I speak out forcefully when members of my family ignore my rights and needs. I no longer spend time with

women who only value shopping and expensive lunches. I left an office job which I didn't need financially and am doing more things that appeal to me. I found out I love weaving and I want to try some other crafts as well."

Even when there has been relatively little conscious reprocessing of painful memories, people report positive results from Mess Painting. It appears that in the altered state of consciousness characteristic of Mess Painting, the inner healer reorganizes material — does self-healing — without the person's conscious knowledge. This is similar to the dreams that we know occurred, but cannot remember on awaking. During sessions without pronounced emotion, trust that the special state of consciousness that is present in Mess Painting is encouraging something positive to occur at a deeper level. Just because nothing is felt, that does not mean that nothing is happening.

Also be aware, however, that if pain, headache, backache, or chest discomfort appear and then persist, they may on rare occasions be due to undiagnosed physical disorders rather than being a sign of self-healing activity. I have rarely met with such situations in the almost twenty years that I have been a CMT facilitator. One exception was George, a transpersonal clinical psychologist in his late twenties, who recognized that certain of his pains had a physical cause: *"Through the painting I came to feel from inside the tension I carry in my throat and chest. Some of that tension is relieved by doing CMT. But I came to sense that the pain in my neck and arm were not due to emotional stuff. I'm finally seeing a chiropractor with good results."* If you tend to believe that all pain is emotionally based, and if painting brings some pain to awareness, please consider the possibility that your body/mind may be calling your attention to a physical problem that may need professional help.

By now it must be apparent that there is no limit to the variety of ways in which people experience Mess Painting. For every ten people who need to unload aggressive, angry feelings before they move into happier moods, there is perhaps one person for whom things proceed in the opposite way. Kathleen, for example, had joyous experiences while painting, as well as the release of negative emotions; but in her case the sessions of ecstasy and freedom occurred before the unloading of rage began:

"I didn't know what CMT would be about. At the beginning of the second session in the second week I was just pushing the paint around on the paper, trying to choose the colors at random. This went on for some time and then abruptly, in the middle of the session, I felt the shift.

"Suddenly I had an understanding that my involvement with the paint and newspaper had nothing to do with caring about how anything looked. I was not there to make a painting, I was there to see what was going to happen — not even to the paper so much, as to myself. It was the jazzy scat singing I was doing that really flipped the light on for me. I just went wild. It felt wonderful. The paint glided by itself over the page — no effort, no thought. Yellow, red, and ultimately the orange they made together. Tri-colored gliding over the page. Where was I? I was seeing it — what 'it' was did not matter.

"I was singing and dancing, really uncontrolled and having an outrageous blast. No one else was home for a change, and I felt absolutely no inhibition. I felt like I was skipping across the newspaper with the brush. I was out of breath — sweating — I was the paint. I went over and locked the door and felt like I was getting away with something and when I saw this feeling, I laughed and laughed. I went on painting until the state of being 'high' left, and then it was okay to go on to the other colors, to blue and purple.

"As I started the second week, I felt as if I had not only found a secret door, but that I actually had a key in my hand and I was beginning to get the gist of how to use it. Such incredibly satisfying freedom to be whoever I was with no fear. I had become like the paper with the paint.

"I thought to myself later: 'So this is what Mess Painting is about. This is so great.' And then, just as week four began, I found myself in a rather uncomfortable, almost depressed state. I now discovered that raw emotions were surfacing in the sessions, in what seemed like a sort of random order. I was, in a word, beginning to lose control. I was particularly disturbed with the anger that kept bubbling up. A part of me began to interfere with the process. One painting would reflect a little anger, the next would be calming and sort of meditative. Then I would be back to anger. I began to experience a considerable amount of frustration, which bled into my life with my family. I was definitely out of sorts, not sleeping well.

"The guidance I received at the weekly meeting at the end of the fourth week was quite important to me, because I gained from it a permission to go into those feelings, to go into what I had been naturally going into and then shying away from. My own psyche was pulling forward what I needed to see or feel. The freedom to listen to this inner voice was helped along by Virginia's encouragement — her coaxing to stay with the feelings, with colors, movements in the body, with sound. After that weekly meeting I really had a sense of needing to trust my natural inclinations. There was no choice involved anymore, or perhaps I should say there was no thinking involved.

"The next session began with intense rage. Words such as 'Bad, bad, bad,' 'I'm dirt,' 'Where are you?' 'Someone needs to help me.' Tension in the throat and eyes, clenched teeth. Hitting the board hard and quick with dark colors of black and red and brown. It felt really wonderful to let myself rage like this and just go to it with no holds barred…. At one point I tore a hole in the paper. That felt really good. After I had the hole torn in that painting, things lightened up for me… very significant that hole. I was really exhausted but at peace when it was over.

"The second session of week five was also very important to me. It was a breakthrough for me — literally. I found myself trapped in sheets of brown and red and blue and feeling more and more claustrophobic. My breathing became very labored and I began to feel a tightness in my throat. The brown was dirt and shit. The trapped feeling was building, building until I couldn't stand it anymore and had to tear a hole in the center of the page. Once I tore the paper I could breathe easier. Once the hole was made I no longer felt trapped. Colors got lighter, air was coming through with the light colors. This exact same process repeated itself for about five paintings. The first torn hole was quite large. Each following page had a progressively smaller tear. And then I discovered I could get the same relief by just leaving an unpainted space in the middle of the painting.

As I worked with overcoming the claustrophobia that came up as I began each painting, I also began to make everything whiter and whiter. I really felt great as this session ended.

"Week number six was very different. In all these sessions, I had the experience of becoming quite unconscious of what I was doing. I remember in one I was on the first sheet of newspaper and then I was on the seventh. What had happened in between them? I saw six drying trays stacked up. I had no recollection of placing a painting on each one. Where had I gone? Later when sharing the paintings I could not say anything about them.

"In the last session, I floated through twenty paintings. Looking at them later I could see they were almost identical, the same colors of light green, white and yellow, the same patterns of brushwork. During the whole session I was very calm, quiet, peaceful and afterwards profoundly relaxed and rested. Although the paintings were so identical, they were not boring to look at. My family and some friends I showed them to were astonished at how beautiful they all were.

"I loved the fact that, except for the few sessions where I interrupted what wanted to happen, I always ended them feeling much better. If I happened to be in a very good mood when I started, I was ecstatic by the time I finished. Being with the colors was so important — I felt as though they were massaging me or satisfying some hunger in my psyche. I found being able to go into a room in my own house, and allow a release to happen, was very healing. I believe that there is a healer within who is, for the most part, non-verbal. At times an intensity of experience is so great that the participant is faced with a challenge to bear these memories and emotions, and may need reassurance from the facilitator that their inner healer will help them. I gradually discovered that I needn't interrupt the kind of raw, painful, out of control emotions that came up. I came to a deep understanding that my inner healer will protect me from undergoing more than I can bear."

The session immediately following Kathleen's early ecstatic one was very disappointing to her. She had expected to have the same freedom, the same "high," and nothing of the sort took place. A really exciting session sets up a strong desire to have another one. However, this desire interferes with having the attitude of passive acceptance necessary for Mess Painting. It is useful to cultivate an open mind, a willingness to allow whatever seems to be happening to have the same importance, or no importance. *Comme si, comme ça,* it's all the same dance.

The Painter Is the Expert

Everyone in Kathleen's CMT group, myself included, was fascinated by her experience of tearing the holes in the newspapers. We piled the five torn paintings on top of each other, looking through the holes to the painting where she had left a space unpainted. As one of the participants said, it was *"like looking through a birth canal."*

Certainly tearing these paintings was of tremendous significance to Kathleen. But it is the act itself that is crucial and healing. Discussing it afterwards — perhaps interpreting it as a ritual act marking the destruction of an old way of being and of moving into something more flexible — is helpful only if the interpretation fits the painter's own conception of what was going on. One of the cardinal principles in CMT is that the person who was there doing the painting is always the final judge of what was happening.

As the facilitator I try to avoid making interpretations or analyzing what I am hearing and seeing. I may ask questions to jog the person's memory of their experience, and I certainly share my emotional reactions to the paintings and point out what seem to be technical errors. My role is always to support the person who is showing his or her paintings, and to help the painter appreciate what was experienced. I am not interested in encouraging the painter or others in the group to intellectualize what the experience was about. As they share their paintings, I remind the participants that each is the final expert on his or her own process — that no one, no facilitator or other group member, has the authority that they do.

CMT is designed to be a win/win situation. As an example, take the problem of boredom. Yes, boring sessions do happen! If you are willing to acknowledge the feeling and nevertheless continue to paint, most of the time the boredom will suddenly be gone and some other feeling will have replaced it.

Sometimes a Mess Painter will do the first five or so paintings and think, *"Gosh, this is boring. I'd rather be doing something else."* And then ten paintings later they wake up to the fifteenth painting — and the last one they remember is number five. This is because they were in an altered state of consciousness. As my client Jenny put it: *"I noticed that I could separate myself from the part of myself that was painting. As my own audience I could think, 'What is she going to do now?' and watch while 'she' did it."*

So be willing to accept boredom for a while. If you've arrived at, say, your eleventh or twelfth painting and you still haven't shifted out of boredom, ask yourself if you are resisting something. If you can honestly say no, then stop Mess Painting and switch over to doing Experimental Painting, as described in the next chapter. This will usually be quite intriguing, and will enable you to feel pleased and satisfied as you end the session.

---

[1] For more information on the CoHousing concept, see Kathryn McCamant and Charles Durrett, *CoHousing*, Ten Speed Press, 1994.

[2] David A. Goodman, *Brain-Mind Bulletin*.

[3] William Frey, *Brain-Mind Bulletin*.

[4] Marie-Louise von Franz, *Creation Myths*, Spring Publications (Zurich), 1972.

Chapter Seven

The Excitement of Something New: Experimental Painting and Beyond

"Improvisation is intuition in action, a way to discover the muse and learn to respond to her call. Even if we work in a very structured, compositional way, we begin by that always surprising process of free invention in which we have nothing to gain and nothing to lose. The outpourings of intuition consist of a continuous, rapid flow of choice, choice, choice, choice. When we improvise with the whole heart, riding this flow, the choices and images open into each other so rapidly that we have no time to get scared and retreat from what intuition is telling us."

- Stephen Nachmanovitch, *Free Play*

Have you felt the magic of CMT yet? After all the hard work of preparation, after careful observance of the rules and dutiful record keeping, are you enjoying the freedom inherent in letting go? Have you emerged from Mess Painting refreshed and energized?

If you are still struggling to let go, be compassionate with yourself. Accept whatever pace your system needs for this process — for this particular curve on your spiral of personal growth. Pat yourself on the back for your diligence, remind yourself that painting without looking for progress is the key, and continue with your commitment.

When you sense the first intimations of the power of Mess Painting to open up positive new feelings of self-worth, it is time to give yourself the excitement of doing something new — namely, Experimental Painting (note the capital E).

Experimental Painting

Experimental Painting is a different experience than the exploratory painting you did at the beginning of your CMT program. During the first week or so you painted with active intention as you enjoyed the materials, familiarized yourself with the paints, brushes, and paper, developed your two-minute time sense, and perhaps encountered some measure of anxiety in the process. Eventually you learned to let go into the Mess Painting experience.

As with Mess Painting, it is very important in the Experimental mode to remain detached from what is appearing on the paper. No praise, no blame continues to be the attitude to cultivate; this will help your inner critic to remain silent. In contrast to Mess Painting, however, Experimental Painting is marked by a state of lightly focused attention. You are invited to make quick, intuitive choices of materials and subject matter, and carry them out. At the same time you are relaxed because you are enjoying the process, are completely absorbed in it, and don't give a hoot about the final result.

In the Experimental mode, you are free of the rules for Mess Painting. Except for the suggestions below as to *when* to do Experimental Painting — a minor restriction of your freedom — it is fair to say that otherwise ANYTHING GOES.

When to Do Experimental Painting

Once you are launched into your Mess Painting adventure and are familiar and at ease with the state of consciousness best described as "letting go," please start Experimental Painting. I encourage you to do one or more Experimental Paintings at the end of your Mess Painting sessions.

You may object to taking time for inventive, playful painting. Why, you may ask, should you do something frivolous? I assure you that involving yourself in the possibilities for fun and surprise will help connect you to your creative self and greatly enrich your CMT experience.

Marty, one of my CMT group members, remarked: *"I had to be told again and again to do the Experimental Paintings at the end of my sessions, or I wouldn't have. But now I always do it. I'm not an artist. In the group I felt like everybody else's Mess Paintings were artistic and mine were ugly. I tricked myself into doing the Experimentals by telling myself I didn't have to show them to anyone."* As we will see later, Marty ended up producing some marvelous Experimental Paintings.

When Emily, the eighty-two-year-old CMT participant mentioned in Chapter 2, produced her delightful landscapes (See Illustration 1, page 129), she was doing Experimental Painting. The preceding Mess Painting session enabled Emily to work intuitively, quickly creating a work of art that expressed her feelings about what she had seen on a recent trip to Canada. Her brush made choices so rapidly that her inner critic could not interrupt the flow of paint to paper.

Mess Painting is not to be followed by Experimental Painting at every session. A highly charged, long, and meaningful Mess Painting session is likely to be sufficient in itself, and the most important thing to do next would be to take a relaxing bath and reflect on what has just happened. However, a traumatic Mess Painting session may so completely finish a piece of old history that the emerging high energy being released will naturally flow into being playful and creative.

Experimental Painting can be particularly gratifying after a boring session, or when there is a feeling of unfinished business and a sense that the session wasn't quite long enough. In these instances some Experimental Painting, perhaps for a longer time than usual, will enable you to leave your work space feeling happy and satisfied. After all, having fun is an important part of this process.

What if you should get a strong desire to do an Experimental Painting at the beginning or during the Mess Painting session? Go ahead and do one, but not more. Then shift back, and pull yourself into the Mess Painting mode immediately. Remember, you will not continue to derive the benefits that come from Mess Painting unless it remains the major focus of your sessions.

Suggestions for the Experimental Painting Mode

Techniques/Materials. Anything goes. There are no rules. You are free to paint as long or as short a time as the painting dictates. Use any colors, choosing them for sheer aesthetic pleasure, allowing them to evoke emotions that may in turn trigger further choices.

In the Experimental mode the paint may be applied in any way — with any size brush, a roller, palette knife, sponge, twigs. Use a paint roller to apply your left-over messy paint to create several backgrounds far more interesting than any paper you could buy.

Spattering can be a technical error during Mess Painting sessions. Now you are free to explore all the possibilities of spattering in your Experimental Paintings. You are also free to use recognizable forms — triangles, stripes, fences, circles.

Explore the power of "What if" — What if I threw this at the paper? What if I used a sponge? What if I smeared the paint around?

Sir George Wade, the Englishman whose experiments with abstract painting were described in Chapter 3, commented:

"It is obvious that if you are going to paint with your subconscious mind, which works at such tremendous speed, you need to use anything at hand as well as brushes . . . fingers, nails, palms, elbows, scrapers, sponges, rags, sandpaper and so on and so on. As the instinct moves you, so you must act, without hesitation, working yourself into a state of rapt enthusiasm, oblivious of time or place until you are in a kind of semi-hypnotic condition which the teenagers used to describe as 'being sent.'

"One thing is certain, if you are going to start this kind of painting you must paint purely for your own satisfaction and never care two hoots for anyone else's criticism. Now I never worry what anyone says, or does not say, about my paintings."

Provide yourself with materials for your Experimental Paintings as though

SUGGESTIONS FOR EXPERIMENTAL PAINTING

- *Anything goes. No rules. No time limit.*

- *Use any kind of paper, any size or shape, and in any position on your board.*

- *Paint beyond the edge of the paper or inside the margins. Create borders.*

- *Fill the entire page or only a small part of it.*

- *Use any kind of paint, any colors, any consistency.*

- *Save dirty paint from Mess Painting sessions and mix it with new colors (magenta, orange, turquoise).*

- *Use very thick paint to produce rough brush strokes.*

- *Drop thick paint into puddles of thin paint.*

- *Mix paint with acrylic gel for a glossy look.*

- *Draw with hot wax, or dribble strands of rubber cement on the paper and paint over it. Melt the wax or peel off the rubber cement to produce bare, unpainted lines. Paint between or over these bare lines. Add sand or plaster for texture.*

- *Press Japanese rice paper on top of a wet Mess Painting. Pull it off and play with the forms on the rice paper after it dries.*

- *Use any size brush, multiple brushes, roller, sponge, palette knife, twigs to apply paint.*

- *Do spattering.*

- *Do fold-overs.*

- *Paint with your hands, fingers, and fingernails.*

- *Paint your dreams, feelings, memories.*

- *Paint landscapes, flowers, portraits, abstract or geometric shapes, mandalas.*

you were an enthusiastic kindergarten teacher collecting materials for her class. The paper can be any kind, and any size — newsprint, butcher paper, water-color paper, rice paper, construction paper. You may use it horizontally, vertically, or diagonally. Cover only a fraction of the paper, or load it down so heavily you can't remove it from your working surface until it has dried a bit.

Use any kind, color, and consistency of paint — left-over house paint, acrylics, oils, gold, silver, crayons, felt-tip pens, marking pens, chalk or oil pastels. Save dirty paint from your earlier Mess Painting sessions and mix it together to produce new colors. Provide yourself with small amounts of other tempera colors, such as magenta, turquoise, and orange. Try adding these to your messy left-over paints.

The original eight colors for Mess Painting have been carefully chosen. It is not helpful to use other colors when you are Mess Painting since they may prove distracting, refocusing your attention on what is appearing on the paper. Extra colors are best used only for your Experimental Paintings. However, on very rare occasions a client has found herself spontaneously incorporating a new color in a Mess Painting session in response to a felt need.

Karen found that combining magenta and white produced a birthday-party pink that could not be obtained by mixing red and white. By using this preferred hue, she was able to relive and enjoy her fourth birthday party all over again. There were no cake, candles, or toys portrayed in the Mess Paintings she made that day, but they all expressed the joy she had experienced long ago.

Fold-Overs. Many of my CMT clients have derived great pleasure and produced some astonishingly beautiful and meaningful paintings by doing fold-overs. Put globs on paint on the newspaper and then fold it over. Wet the paper with a random application of paint, or pour paint directly onto the paper and smear it around. While folding and unfolding the paper, add more paint. Your paint splotches may turn into mysterious images of mythical creatures, of worldly places or heavenly architecture.

Sandra, a middle-aged woman from a large Catholic family, did a very beautiful fold-over that looked like a cathedral partly covered by mist. Her husband, a church architect, framed the painting and put it in his office. Janice Crow, an artist whose CMT experiences are described in the next chapter, experienced a powerful spiritual awakening through her interaction with a fold-over painting that appeared to be a shamanic figure.

Finger Painting. Break all the Mess Painting Rules. Use several brushes at the same time. Paint with your fingers, or your feet. Smear the paint on with your hands. After building up thick layers of paint, use your fingers and fingernails to create marvelous patterns that expose layers of paint of various colors (See Illustration 4, page 129). Some fastidious people prefer to wear tight-fitting surgical gloves for this.

Ann Keiffer, who in Chapter 3 described her initial intimidation with art materials, found painting with her bare hands to be the most rewarding part of her entire CMT experience:

"When I began, I would Mess Paint twenty or so paintings, then switch to Experimentals. I tended to paint 'things' — not a still-life nor the perfect pear with a wedge of cheese, but images from my dreams or meaningful symbols: a teapot, a tomato, a broken crown. Even that was exciting. And once when one of the images from a painting actually surfaced in a dream a few nights later, I knew my outer and inner lives were conversing through this process.

"Then an even more interesting thing happened. I began to notice this insistent, persistent compulsion to get my hands in the paint. It seemed silly, like finger-painting, back to kindergarten, really low on the artistic totem pole. But I had to. So I began to experiment, allowing myself to smear, stroke, pat, push, smoosh the paint around with my fingers and hands. No longer bound to painting things, I experimented with the sensual experience of painting itself. I watched two colors come together to make a third color and felt as if I'd seen the face of God. I felt the paint move not just on the page, but in my belly. I painted blobs and layers of color and dragged my fingers through them for the joy of the mystery that would emerge. I created wild, exploding Medusa-like mandalas; clouds of color; fireworks of intensity; unintended skies full of exploding stars. Painting in this way has been the

fulfillment of the sensation of wet paint on my hands. Perhaps my feet are next. As I move my hands over the paper, I am in communion with my life, my life as I want it to be: a handmade life filled with all the richness of experience, color and mystery."

There is no requirement that you try out all the possible ways of doing Experimental Painting unless you want to. Many people discover one or two things that they prefer to do, and then explore all the possibilities of those approaches. They may use one idea again and again just because they find it so satisfying. If you want to try something in an Experimental Painting that hasn't been suggested here, by all means go ahead and do it.

Content. Experimental Paintings can have any subject matter, or can be abstract. Paint flower arrangements or landscapes from memory, or paint dream images. Try a self-portrait, or the portrait of a teacher you hated, or a favorite childhood doll, toy, or truck.

Emily tried a number of approaches in her Experimental Paintings, and then settled exclusively on doing landscapes. Peter, a robust man who is skilled in the building trades, painted exquisite flowers (See Illustration 10, page 130). Sometimes the flowers were very large, with only two or three of them filling the entire newspaper. Other times the flowers were so delicate and small that it took a great many of them to cover the paper. These paintings could easily be used as designs for gorgeous silk fabrics.

Insights, Dreams, and Feelings. Many CMT participants paint their dreams. Your Dream Diary can be a rich resource of material that may emerge in Experimental Paintings.

Marty did her second CMT program fifteen years after the first. This second time, she created a permanent setup where she could continue Mess Painting as needed to unload the debris of ordinary life — and also continue with the regular painting of her dreams. It has not surprised me to see an artist set aside a corner of her studio for Mess Painting. But when someone who is not a professional artist devotes precious space in a small apartment to a permanent Mess Painting setup, I am reminded how important CMT can be in fitting some individuals' needs.

In two different sessions, five days apart, Marty created two paintings of the same dream, shown in Illustrations 5 and 6 on page 129. Marty describes the dream as follows:

"I was in the water with three Orca whales, training them to jump and flip in the water. I showed them a flip in which I jumped out of the water, turned upside down and fell back into the water. Then the whales did this really easily, and asked me: 'Did you touch bottom?' I realized then that they already knew how to do it all along, and that I didn't touch the bottom and they did. I was so embarrassed — here I was training them, and they knew how to do it better all along."

Marty had badly injured an arm at her previous job, and as a result was seeing several therapists. The first Orca painting was done as an Experimental at the end of a rather cerebral Mess Painting session, during which she decided to stop seeing a body worker about whom she had some reservations.

With this decision made and the Mess Painting session feeling complete, Marty did the first Experimental Painting of the Orca whales:

"I think I had the idea that if I were going to create an image, I should be able to think of it and then do it, and it should kind of look like what I was thinking — it should appear as it did in my mind's eye. But since I can't draw, the Experimentals wouldn't come out that way at all. I was dissatisfied with the first Orca painting because there was no motion — the whole thing about the dream was all the motion. It was interesting to do it though, because I really had no idea how to do it — it's amazing how a part of the brain seems to take over and you kind of have to stand out of the way.

"I wanted to do another Orca Experimental. The next session was five days later, and I didn't know ahead of time that I would do it then. That session was very angry and emotional — one of the ones about my rage and frustration at a dying friend. I was very irritated; during that week I had met with her and had a very unpleasant time. She later apologized but it wasn't enough; I really wanted to get away from her. I kept thinking while I was painting, 'I'm mired in the muck, I'm mired in the muck.' All the Mess Paintings were very muddy looking

— *mired in the muck. Several of the Mess Paintings preceding the three Orcas, in red and black and brown, are crumpled and torn.*

"*I didn't even know what I was doing when I was painting the three Orcas. And they came out completely different from my first attempt — completely free, so spontaneous and easy and full of motion. Later when looking at this painting I realized that art is a whole different process than what I thought it was, it is about learning to relax and just see what will happen next.*

"*I also realized that both of the sessions before the Orca Experimentals were about needing to get away from people who I was experiencing as toxic to me. I find now that I am seeing my difficult friend much less. I am planning other things to do on the weekends, not leaving time open for her to plan something with me at the last minute if she is feeling well enough — and not feeling guilty about this. So both the Experimental and the Mess Painting were useful in working some of that out.*"

Recognizing the emotional impact of your Mess Paintings, you have probably begun to get some ideas about how feelings can be expressed in painting. Kathy Goss, one of my editors, translated an emotionally charged insight from a Mess Painting session into an Experimental self-portrait:

"*I did a very important Mess Painting series in which I had a spontaneous memory of my mother making me write 100 times, 'I will be a decent girl,' when I did a prank of dropping my shorts in front of my little playmates. I was a decent girl. As I painted I felt rage: 'All right, Mommy, I'll show you. I'll be decent. I won't be popular. I'll be fat. I won't get married and have babies. Feed me, keep me fat.' I remembered her sneaking into my bedroom one night, years later, and tiptoeing out with my purse to read my letters. I never forgave her for this betrayal of trust. Why didn't she trust me?*

"*At the end of this session I did an Experimental Painting of myself as a plump child with a sad, vacant look in my eyes, entitled 'Eat Your Dessert, Dear.' This was my first painting of a person during my CMT program. I thought I couldn't paint figures, but this was charming, and everyone in the group knew what it was, right down to the strawberry shortcake and the African violets.*"

Mandalas. Many CMT painters have enjoyed doing mandalas in their Experimental Painting time. It was the Swiss psychiatrist Carl Jung who adopted the Sanskrit word *Mandala* to describe the circle drawings that he and his patients produced. Jung associated the mandala with the self, the center of the total personality.

As described by Jung, a mandala might be circular, spherical, or egg-shaped, or elaborated into a flower or wheel design. At the center might be a sun, a star, a cross, generally with four, eight, or twelve rays. It might be represented by a snake coiled around a center, as in the ring-shaped uroboros, or the spiral of the Orphic egg. The circle might be placed in a square, or a square in a circle.

Lynne derived much comfort from doing mandalas at the end of most of her sessions:

"I purchased several books in preparation for doing CMT, among them Jung's Memories, Dreams and Reflections, and Jose Arguelles' Mandala. Doing mandalas became my favorite thing. Since I am often in meetings that require only light concentration, I now draw mandalas while sitting there. I look at the empty circle and there comes a sense of what I want to put down. The whole thing evolves bit by bit."

Bruce, a financial consultant with a muscular build, made egg-like mandalas in almost every session. Mandala after mandala appeared along with the Mess Paintings — great oval shapes that covered the entire work surface. If he did another immediately after the first, which he generally did (if not six or seven more), he pulled the paint left on the board onto the as yet unpainted newspaper and went on from there (See Illustration 8, page 130). Each mandala painting, even though so huge and having so many colors and coats of paint, took him only about four or five minutes. Adding up the mandalas he produced in two successive CMT groups, Bruce estimates that he made over a hundred. The act of painting them was an important part of his CMT experience.

Jack, the environmental lawyer quoted in Chapter 6, was attending Dr.

Stanislav Grof's Holotropic Breathwork sessions on an ongoing basis. Grof's participants are requested to create mandalas at the end of each breathwork session. Jack had always been frustrated and a bit angry when asked to do this, but after his Mess Painting program his resistance to doing mandalas vanished. He treated them as he had his Mess Paintings, choosing colors emotionally and letting the mandala happen on its own. Previously he had assumed that he should be able to create an image in his mind of what his breathing experience had meant and put it full blown on paper. Now he just lets it evolve.

The power of mandalas to express the whole self in a very simple form is reminiscent of an art form pursued by Zen Buddhist artist-priests, as described by musician-author Stephen Nachmanovitch in his book *Free Play*:

"Some of the artwork we particularly remember them for are their ensos, those portraits of mind and reality that consist of nothing but an O, a circle brushed on paper with a single stroke. There's more to that 'nothing but' than meets the eye. The character of that O, the variations and bends of the curve, its weights and textures, its wiggles and blemishes, reveal an imprimatur that comes from a place much deeper than the style of the time, much deeper than technical ability or the surface of personality."

The Pleasure and Empowerment of Painting

CMT participants often feel a strong sense of self-affirmation when they discover their ability to paint. Many echo the sentiments expressed by Joan, who loved the way she felt while doing her later Experimental Paintings: *"It's very empowering to see yourself as an artist."*

While professional artists are generally not quite so vocal in appreciating their own work, many people who paint as an avocation are not at all reticent about expressing their admiration of their improvisations. Novelist Henry Miller unabashedly described his love affair with his watercolor paintings:

"Occasionally I will paint after I have done my stint of writing for the day.... Sooner or later, however, the writing drags me back to my desk. Now comes

an equally exciting period, one in which I seize any and every opportunity to court my paintings. Stealing away from the typewriter, I sneak up on them and gaze in amazement. (Did I really do that... and that? How?) In this mood, which fortunately doesn't last forever, I'd rather stare at my own poor efforts than at a Picasso, a Vermeer, or even a Hokusai. The only artists for whom I would make way are — children. For me the paintings of children belong side by side with the works of the masters.... The work of a child never fails to make appeal, to claim us, because it is always honest and sincere, always imbued with that magic certitude born of the direct, spontaneous approach."

Beyond Experimental Painting

In his description of CMT Luthe includes a third, much more elusive kind of painting, which he describes as Self-Evolving Painting. Perhaps the best way to begin to characterize these paintings is to return to Marty's experience in painting her Orca dream.

Her first painting (Illustration 5, page 129) depicts the subject matter of the dream. Here Marty makes a brave attempt to paint a whale and produce the texture of splashing water. This is easily categorized as an Experimental Painting.

What happened with the second picture of the Orcas (Illustration 6, page 129) is something that frequently happens to other CMT painters also. Marty's Mess Painting session had been extremely emotional and very satisfying. Tearing holes and crumpling the last three paintings left her open, relaxed, full of energy, and with feelings of personal freedom that she carried into the time for play and improvisation. The resulting painting, intended as an Experimental, somehow moved beyond this category into something special.

In the group meeting everyone responded to the emotional impact of this painting — to the delight, spontaneity and freedom it expressed. This kind of response from others, or from oneself, is often the mark of a painting intended to be a Mess Painting or Experimental Painting, which has unexpectedly become what Luthe has described as Self-Evolving.

Special Awareness and Special Impact. Through her experience with this second painting, Marty discovered that art was quite a different process than she had imagined – that it entailed *"relaxing and seeing what will happen next."*

Bruce described a similar experience with his mandala paintings:

"I slowed down when I did the mandalas, though I never started a painting with the intention of painting one — they always just evolved. I would find myself in the first thirty to forty seconds of a painting, I could feel it taking shape and there was a magnetic pole which pulled me toward continuing it as a mandala. At that point I would be in conflict: I'd have to give up my desire to Mess Paint. Then I'd let myself go into it and once I accepted I was going to paint one, it felt right and it was very peaceful. When I look at them later, there is something that just resonates, it is a part of me — a deep inner mysterious part."

Luthe in his textbook instructs CMT participants to interrupt their Mess Painting sessions to do one or two Self-Evolving Paintings — that is, to do paintings in which they consciously allow the painting to take them in a direction in which it seems to be going — enhancing, joining with, and expanding on the colors and forms on the newspaper.

Because I feel a strong obligation to present CMT as close to Luthe's design as possible, until recently I conscientiously gave my groups his instructions for doing Self-Evolving Paintings. I followed his model even though, when he was my guide, I wrote in my notes: *"Now that I know about Self-Evolving Painting my sessions are less fun. Interrupting Mess Painting to do a Self-Evolving one spoils the rhythm and flow of the session."*

I am sure that Luthe's efforts to create a category called Self-Evolving Painting came from his recognition that during the weeks of a CMT program everyone created paintings that had expressive and aesthetic qualities that spoke to viewers in profound ways. These paintings were so special that they called out to be noticed, perhaps by a separate categorization.

In my experience — and I am sure in Luthe's as well — often the person who did such a painting was not at all aware of its specialness until others, on seeing it, responded with a gasp of surprise, a clap of the hands, words of appreciation, or some other acknowledgment.

I remember the first time one of my paintings received such recognition. Luthe reached out for the painting, removing it from the family of Mess Paintings of which it was a part, and placed it behind glass in a handsome gold frame. I was astonished at what I saw. There was a beauty in the rhythm of strokes, in the texture, in the use of color. The following week, Luthe provided me once again with the same joy and feeling of empowerment when he honored what had begun as an Experimental Painting by placing it in the gold frame behind mat and glass. In both instances I believe that as I painted I was not only undergoing an optimal experience of absorption in a process, with no thought of product, no thought of self, but that in addition some hidden part of my psyche was guiding my brush.

Those paintings of mine, and all the rare and special ones by others that I have been fortunate to witness, could be called Self-Evolving, but over time I have become tempted to search for another word. Self-Evolving doesn't fully describe what I experience when I see one of these special paintings. Each one has arisen out the Mess Painting or Experimental mode, and owes its existence to the extensive practice of these two kinds of painting. Each one has transcended the act and the category of Mess Painting or Experimental Painting.

So, rather than use Luthe's term, I prefer transcendental. I think of such paintings as transcending the others the person has done. These paintings happen spontaneously — more of them for some people than for others. It seems a contradiction of the underlying premise of CMT to contrive to make such paintings happen. I should like to have the opportunity some day to discuss this point with others who studied with Luthe.

I have mentioned that these special paintings, whether done during Mess Painting or Experimental time, are often first identified by another person or by the whole group at a weekly meeting. These paintings arouse a strong emotional response of pleasure and excitement, or of harmony and transcendence, in the viewer. The painter may be quite surprised at the depth of response.

Such was the experience of Brad, a young businessman who was so ambivalent and anxious about dealing with art materials that he was willing to pay me to help him create his painting space. In my visit to his home, while looking at the paintings that an interior decorator had chosen for him, I remarked that one day I would be helping him frame one of his Mess Paintings — and that he would enjoy looking at it more than any that were hanging up now. Brad assured me that couldn't possibly happen since he didn't have the slightest artistic ability.

Brad had happened to join a CMT group in which there were three artists. He was taking CMT as a way of helping himself to deal with his father's death, and in experiencing his grief while Mess Painting he scarcely noticed his paintings, even when he was removing them from the drying trays.

So it was with utter amazement that Brad watched the artists gather over a painting of his now and then, exclaiming *"Look at that!"*, *"Wow, how did he do that?"*, *"Isn't this one lovely!"* Much later, long after CMT had ended, Brad told me that my prediction had come true: *"Looking at the painting I had framed and put up on my wall gives me a sense of empowerment. I really enjoy it and knowing it came out of me... well, what can I say?"*

Clearly, categorizing paintings in CMT is not an exact science. But it is worthwhile to make an effort to separate them, or you may contaminate the Mess Painting process itself. By helping you to recognize and appreciate the subtle differences in awareness that are present in the different painting modes, your CMT program can help you to develop and carry out creative ideas in other areas of your life. Some states of consciousness are conducive to originating an idea or invention, while others are needed for the actualization part of the creative process.

How Special Paintings Evolve. While creating one of these special paintings, the painter is typically in a deep meditative state. Painter and painting are so fused, the painter is so at ease with the act of painting, that there is no consciousness of a momentary shift out of indifference into a detached interest in what is forming on the paper. It is as though the brush strokes are painting themselves from some primal ground. "Breathing something more into a Mess Painting" is one way of describing what takes place.

It is possible that in the course of a Mess Painting session you may occasionally feel moved to take one of the paintings further in the direction it seems to want to go. If you do that, the rules for Mess Painting are temporarily relaxed. The two-minute rule is suspended, and you may take as much time as you wish on the painting. An inner, intuitive relationship with the painting will dictate just the right moment to stop and place the work to dry. You may also include subject matter in the painting. The Mess Painting strokes already on the paper may suggest an animal, a dancing figure, a landscape. If you remain completely absorbed in the painting process, your mind will not be busy making judgments about the effectiveness of your strokes, or thinking about making something that will be pleasing to others or yourself.

As one of these special paintings is evolving, it may feel as if your hand is being guided from a source outside yourself. The impulse to add a color here, a brush stroke there, may seem to be coming from somewhere else, rather than being a decision formed in your own thoughts.

As your painting appears on the paper, your ego may feel gratification at this new possibility for creating striking paintings, and you may want to produce more. Beware of such temptations. Without maintaining an attitude of openness, with no expectations, no goals, the CMT process deteriorates and loses its beneficial power.

It is crucial, at the moment you wet the work surface for the next piece of newspaper, that you say to your brain, <u>out loud</u>: *"Brain, that was fine, and we enjoyed that. But now let's return to Mess Painting, and pay no attention to what is appearing on the paper. The next time we see something that appeals to us we will not respond to it, or paint around that area, or in any way attempt to save it."*

This kind of self-talk may also be necessary at the beginning of your next painting session. It is only human to attempt to repeat very satisfying experiences, but in this case that will not be helpful. You must reject the desire to make another extraordinary painting. Please follow this piece of advice, or you will soon find yourself caught up in ego-centered product making.

Mess Painting requires a carefully defined structure. If you find yourself deviating from that structure, please recognize that you are doing so. Fully acknowledge that you are deviating, and go ahead without self-reproach. But don't deceive yourself into thinking that you have done a Mess Painting session, if in fact you have been doing Experimental Painting. Mess Painting brings very special benefits of self-discovery that cannot be obtained when ignoring its rules.

Our states of consciousness are very subtle and discrete, and the better you can develop your sense of the differences, the better you will be able to apply this awareness in your everyday life.

Affinity with Abstract Expressionism

CMT painters often discover when they visit museums that they feel a powerful connection with Abstract Expressionist painting. The unbounded, expansive, emotional approach that characterizes Abstract Expressionism is reminiscent of the freely expressive quality of Mess Painting.

Susan Landauer, in her book *The San Francisco School of Abstract Expressionism,* says that the Abstract Expressionists *"saw Art as an experience of adventure, discovery and evolving consciousness."* Once they are at home with the process, CMT painters see Mess Painting in the same way.

Perhaps my early grounding in the lively, exciting San Francisco art scene is part of the reason that I find CMT so appealing. When I first arrived in California, no one in the Bay Area was describing themselves as Abstract Expressionists; they were simply painting. That's what Mess Painters are also doing — simply painting. If they are professional artists, they are discovering through CMT that they have a whole new way to tap into their creativity, possibly to make changes in their technique, to feel free to do whatever they please. For individuals who have never painted, CMT shows them how it feels to be an artist, which can be a very self-affirming experience.

The Abstract Expressionists were concerned with freedom and conveying emotions. Similarly, it is the emotional impact of CMT paintings, even those by non-artists, that gives them their strong appeal and explains why even unschooled painters have been able to produce powerful paintings.

Because its emotional truthfulness comes from deep within the self, the CMT painting process can carry participants into realms beyond ordinary consciousness. For many CMT participants, the last turn of the spiral is the opening of a door into a transcendent, spiritual realm — a realm that is somehow captured in wonderful, mysterious paintings that are capable of creating a similar opening for those who see them.

Such transcendent experiences, and their transformative effects on the lives of CMT participants, are the subject of the next chapter.

Chapter Eight

Painting into Transcendence

"If anything, art could provide an equivalent for what in the East is called meditation; and there is perhaps nothing we need more urgently at a time when aimless perfection of technical means has become self-destructive."

- Wolfgang Paalen, *Metaplastic*

It took several years to prepare this book for publication. Even as I was reaching the home stretch in revising the manuscript, there was a long interruption just before I began work on the final two chapters. A number of dramatic events stopped the writing process — the violent death of my editor's housemate; my own incapacitation with a hip fracture; and then, after my recovery from the injury, the arduous task of selling my home of 27 years and moving from 2000 square feet to a tiny apartment of 500 square feet.

As it turned out, this long and sometimes frustrating delay had a fortunate conclusion. Although there were already rough drafts of the final two chapters, I had not been happy with them. They seemed so pedestrian and boring when compared to the excitement I felt about CMT. The interruption forced me to take a broader view of the meaning and purpose of this book. Having come face to face with the facts of mortality, I was propelled into a greater interest in spiritual growth, and came to appreciate fully the role of CMT in such a growth process.

At the same time, in an unrelated development, Susan Landauer's book, *The San Francisco School of Abstract Expressionism*, mentioned in the previous chapter, appeared in the bookstores. This book richly documents the period when I arrived in California and first encountered the vibrant art world of San Francisco, just when the city was beginning to recognize the importance of modern art. Paging through the book, I relived the excitement that filled the air at that time. Those were the days of the first and only sit-down strike at an art museum. I happened to be part of the large crowd that refused to leave the Museum of Modern Art at the closing hour of 10 p.m. on the final evening of a Picasso exhibit, forcing the Museum to stay open beyond midnight until we had had our fill. Looking at the reproductions in Landauer's book, I was struck by the similarity of some special CMT paintings to the feeling of freedom, the emotional impact, and the spiritual power of Abstract Expressionist art.

Eventually I returned to my writing task and tried to pick up the thread of my narrative. As I reviewed the written reports of clients and my own notes from CMT group meetings, I was impressed by how many people had reported unusual, transcendent experiences while doing Mess Painting — not to mention those soaring moments when they produced the special paintings that Luthe would have labeled Self-Evolving.

The changes in my own life and needs, as well as my observations about the openings in awareness experienced by CMT participants, reminded me that there is another dimension to CMT, another turn of the spiral. In fact, for some Mess Painters the CMT experience can be predominantly spiritual in nature.

CMT as Spiritual Retreat

For me the most memorable example of a profoundly spiritual CMT experience was that of Father Dunstan Morrissey. Having this man come into one of my groups was one of the most remarkable encounters that I have had in facilitating CMT. Drawing a deep, awestruck inner breath, I asked myself, "Why would such a person, with his accomplishments, be interested in participating in a CMT group?"

When Dunstan joined my group in the spring of 1988, I had already learned of his unusual history from our mutual friends, artists Janice Crow and John Curry. He had felt a spiritual calling at an early age, and became a Catholic when a senior in college, convinced even then that his true vocation would be as a monk. After graduation, just before reporting for duty with the Foreign Service, he had a mystical experience that confirmed his resolution to pursue a religious life. After two years' duty as vice consul in Alexandria, Egypt, Dunstan left to become a Benedictine monk and Catholic scholar.

Having lived fifteen years in community in a Benedictine monastery, Dunstan was finally given permission to enter a life of solitude — a traditional practice among the Benedictine order until the French Revolution, revived by the Church in the 1960s.

For four years, Dunstan lived in solitude, first on the island of Martinique and then on Vancouver Island, his only human contact being with his spiritual director at intervals as long as six weeks. Today he lives a monastic life at Sky Farm, a spiritual retreat center he created in Sonoma County, California.

Saint Benedict described the practice of the "Solitaire Benedictine" as doing *"single-handed combat in the desert, that is, in solitude."* Dunstan considers the path of solitude to be roughly comparable to the path of pure research among scientists — a state of wide-open exploration with no immediate utilitarian goal or focus: *"In society there are all these things that keep our attention . . . but in solitude, we have to confront ourselves, and face the unconscious directly, and that is combat."*

Perhaps the fact that CMT is an experience in solitude contributed to Dunstan's decision to try it out. But what, I wondered, could Mess Painting possibly do for Dunstan? Would he find it trivial and superficial?

I needn't have wondered. For Dunstan it was a case of perfect timing. He had been going through an unpropitious period in his life, fraught with many difficulties. And unbeknownst to me, Dunstan had already distinguished himself as an artist, having studied with the famed potter Marguerite Wildenhain after he was instructed by his bishop to return to society. An exacting teacher, Wildenhain insisted that her students make five thousand pots and throw them away before they present a pot to the public. For two years Dunstan worked as a janitor at night and spent his days throwing pots and destroying them, making his 5000 pots. After that he made pots that he sold.

In one Mess Painting session, about three or four weeks into the process, Dunstan began to paint crosses (See Illustration 7, page 130) in the midst of a flow of passionate energy. An intoxication with color and more color had permeated the session, suddenly exploding into the image of a huge cross that filled an entire sheet of newspaper. Another cross and another came forth, glowing as no previous work had done. The crosses flew onto the paper from the core of Dunstan's being. Had a car backfired or a thunderstorm erupted, he would not have noticed. The crosses were within him, and he was inside the crosses; there was no sense of self and other.

In another painting session, images of the East emerged in Dunstan's paintings. Without conscious volition, his rhythmic brush work moved away from the anonymity of Mess Painting as though with a purpose of its own, making large, broad strokes suggestive of Japanese calligraphy (See Illustration 9, page 130). Both the crosses and the calligraphic images appeared again on other days, and were as great a surprise each time.

Even though Dunstan had shifted in these paintings from formless, messy painting to discernible content, all of the mental, physical, and executional aspects of Mess Painting were still operating. The images that emerged onto the newspapers reflected the two primary interests of his lifetime — his practice and study of Catholicism, and his extensive study of Oriental philosophy — first Zen with Suzuki Roshi, and later an extensive study in an ashram in India of the Upanishads, the Bhavagad Gita, and the Brahma Sutras, which required him to learn Sanskrit.

At the end of his eight weeks of painting, Dunstan told me how profoundly his CMT experience had affected him:

"There was a great opening of the unconscious, delineating a certain path in my life. As I see it now, I think of it as a way of affirming the depth and the validity of the interests that I've followed through my life. It was wonderful to me because then I realized that these interests that I'd pursued weren't arbitrary; they sprang from some deep place within me. It was as if I were touching the ORIGIN of those interests; that's the way it was. That's how I felt.

"And all that came up arbitrarily to me — I didn't set out to paint a cross, you know, or those calligraphic brush strokes. I have been deeply drawn to the convergence of East and West most of my life, and the cross, well, to me it just grows in importance right to this day, it's central — but to have it revealed through my own unconscious, this was another thing.

"That these two clusters of imagery reflect the conscious interests of a lifetime indicates the unity of the mind. To see this is to see that the distinctions between the 'conscious' and the 'unconscious' are imposed upon the mind by a fragment of itself. In my identification with the 'thinking I,' I exist brokenly. CMT allowed for a certain unifying understanding of the real in my personal life."

With humility, I welcomed Dunstan's comments on the impact that CMT had had on him:

"I wouldn't recommend it to anybody who just wants to pile onto their agenda another workshop, or to anybody who just wanted to paint some pretty pictures, just to express themselves. But I would recommend it to anyone I felt was really concerned with tracing in themselves the authentic, anyone who was deeply concerned with self-knowledge."

When living in solitude, Dunstan had adhered to a strict schedule with obedience to structure. And so he could appreciate the structure in CMT:

"The poet Robert Frost said once, 'You can't play tennis without nets.' The net in CMT is the structure; it creates a situation — a solitude — within which to find those parts of yourself that need tending. There is also the possibility, in a carefully structured solitude, of experiencing a transcendence of the dualities and

of encountering non-ordinary realities."

Who better than Dunstan Morrissey would be able to appreciate the value of the private space, the solitude, that CMT requires?

Many Facets of Spirituality

I do not mean to imply that only a person of such spiritual depth as Dunstan Morrissey could have been capable of transcendent experiences during the CMT program. Much of this book has been concerned with practical matters — preparation for Mess Painting, the detailed instructions for creating and dealing with the paintings. But, once the practical matters have been handled, much higher up on the spiral, Mess Painting can lead to an expansion of awareness.

Spirituality has taken many forms in the experience of CMT participants — awareness of non-ordinary reality; reaffirmation of one's traditional faith (as in the case of Susan, described in Chapter 1, who shared the Passover Seder with her son); confrontations with death; experiences of self-healing, self-acceptance, and profound insights; the embracing of solitude; a feeling of oneness with the universe; and an expansive lightness of being such as that experienced by Gay Luce while creating her marvelous paintings (See Illustration, 12 page 132).

Progressive Growth Through Repeated CMT Programs

Artist Janice Crow has experienced many of these facets of spirituality in the course of her long involvement with CMT. Janice and her husband, sculptor/painter John Curry, have maintained a rewarding artistic and personal relationship for more than twenty years. Their partnership began with a very successful pottery studio; in fact, their work has been acquired by collectors all over the world. Later, first John and then Janice built their own studios, and more recently they created a gracious, art-filled bed-and-breakfast inn on their property in Sonoma County.

It was not until she did CMT, however, that Janice was first able to acknowledge her identity as a painter. Even though she had a fine arts degree, considered herself a master potter, had been painting for years, and had exhibited both ceramics and paintings, Janice always considered herself a student when it came to painting:

"In 1984, following my first exposure to Mess Painting, I had gained enough self-assurance to study with a renowned artist, Wayne Thiebaud. That initial experience with CMT in 1984 also gave me the confidence I needed to expand the size of my watercolors. I began to use three-and-a-half by five foot paper. I'm a small person, but I love working on a large scale."

Through her studies with Thiebaud, Janice came to realize that she really was a painter, rather than just being a student trying to learn how to paint. Then, through her second Mess Painting program, she continued her artistic development:

"After my second encounter with Mess Painting in 1986 I began to paint with acrylics and oil on canvas, and my increasing range of expression began to develop into a more personal and autobiographical style. In 1987, I started a series of drawings and watercolors from childhood snapshots. This series, which still interests me and has recently brought me commissions, combines an image with a word and a definition of that word.

"For instance, a drawing made from a snapshot of me at age three shows an honest, resolute child standing erect and looking straight ahead. Above the child, printed in large letters, are the words, 'Integrity: perfect unbroken condition.' I feel that that three-year-old is an essence or part of me that is whole and still lives at the core of my being."

Janice is convinced that she would not have made these developments in her personal painting style and her inner growth if she hadn't done Mess Painting more than one time. Each of her experiences with Mess Painting has been unique:

"During my second Mess Painting course, an image appeared in a painting which to me had the feeling of a feathered, birdlike being. A few days later, I came across an article which spoke directly to me, interpreting the image I had painted.

I had always been an avid student, taking classes to learn, but not confident in my own self-knowledge. The main point of the article was to trust our inner knowing. It described the feathered shaman as the symbol of a realized being who has embodied that knowledge. The article stated:

> *"'In ancient Ecuadorian culture the spirit was pictured as a feathered shaman, dancing with rattle in hand. The emphasis was on birdlike flight of the spirit as well as rhythmic movement and music. The goal of the shaman was to fly beyond all boundaries, to come into firsthand encounter with the visible and invisible dimensions of nature.*
>
> *"'Shamanism is basically a stategy for personal learning and for acting on that learning. The only thing a teacher can do is get you started with the methods. If you are really going to be a shaman, you are going to learn directly from your own experiences. These are incredibly revelatory experiences, filled with information, and that is where the real learning takes place. Your experience will be your true teacher.'"*

Janice had no idea at the time that two years later, during her third CMT experience, the feathered being would reappear, with life-changing consequences.

In 1988, during some six sessions in her third CMT program, Janice found herself covering sheet after sheet with only black paint, as I have described in Chapter 2. Although fully aware of the instructions to use several colors in each painting, she found it impossible to use any color except black. Finally she found herself painting black bars. The shape of the bars triggered a childhood memory of being left alone in her playpen hour after hour, without attention to her needs, and of being beaten if she cried, made any noise, or protested in any way.

Still working with the black paint, Janice began an Experimental fold-over painting (See Illustration 3, page 129):

"At the end of this intensely cathartic Mess Painting session I started an

Experimental Painting. After blanketing the newspaper with black paint, I began adding red and white. I believe I was moved by something beyond ordinary consciousness in the way I added these colors and did the fold-overs. As I finished I could see black feathers, as well as what looked like a shaman. The appearance of the feathers planted the image of my maiden name 'Crow' in me — a name I lost when I was only seventeen and I married for the first time. Ever since that day of Mess Painting, I have signed my work 'Janice Crow.' I framed this cherished painting, which I called the 'Dark Angel,' and included it as part of my large retrospective exhibit in Tiburon, California in 1995."

It seems to me that Janice was going through a "dark night of the soul," and the Dark Angel led her out of the despair that was still festering in her forgotten memory of being confined to a playpen without stimulation or emotional sustenance. Recovering this preverbal memory allowed Janice to recognize how she had been suppressing her own power throughout her life. Then in the next series of paintings the feathered dark shaman emerged. It was as if a powerful part of herself was coming through to be born, expressed, and acknowledged once again.

Janice's involvement with CMT took still another turn of the spiral in 1996. For years she had felt strongly that CMT should be made more widely available, but she had never thought of herself as the person to do it. After going through four formal CMT programs over an eleven- or twelve-year period, as well as many other trainings in awareness and growth techniques during that time, Janice organized a group for me to lead in 1996. Before we could begin, I suffered my hip injury and was unable to lead the group. The members of the group suggested that perhaps Janice could lead it. I confirmed that she could, with supervision from me. Deciding that she had the free time to lead the group just then, Janice undertook it:

"What I love about this technique is that I give people the tools, the materials, and the structure of rules to follow. I facilitate their process as it develops on its own, being careful not to interfere with that unfolding by interpreting or analyzing. I am part of the structure that allows people to teach themselves — to inform themselves,

on whatever level necessary, about whatever they need to be informed of. For them and for me, it's like opening a surprise package."

Transcending Time, Space, and Death. Elaine blossomed into a painter after doing CMT with me in 1978. In 1979 she had an exhibit of her paintings at the Southern Exposure Gallery in San Francisco. In her artist's statement for the show, Elaine said:

"These works are works of the spirit. They are intuitive and their inner logic is emotional. The search is continuous for symbols that evoke the power of inner life. They make connections with the world of primitive art.

"These paintings evolved after spending two months practicing the CMT technique early in 1978. CMT opened the door of my unconscious and allowed me to get in touch with a deeper level of myself. The works of C.G. Jung helped in the understanding of the symbols that have spontaneously emerged."

During her CMT program, Elaine had an unusual experience of contacting her son, who had died many years earlier:

"I was very upset as a result of a heavy argument the night before and felt isolated, without anyone.

"I started by humming and singing 'La Vie en Rose,' 'Around the World in 80 Days.' This feeling of anguish intensified as I began 'My Buddy.' I thought of our son who died thirteen years ago at age 24 — so brilliant, so brave. We had a special relationship. I said I missed him and loved him. I realized that he was just above me, a little to the right, mostly white light, his face blurred a little. He knew I had called him for help and he stayed quite close. I was crying or sobbing all the time.

"I was happy to see him and to know that he would help me develop my painting. He said that when I needed him I should call to him and I got the feeling that he felt I should have known to ask him before this. He said he would help all the family if they asked him."

Some weeks later, on Good Friday, Elaine again experienced contact with her son:

"I felt fine, very high, a good night's sleep, a beautiful day. Very soon I felt a

feeling of great love. I was crying. I miss you. I love you. Jimmy was in the same space. I had a feeling of reaching for help and a sensation in my stomach. I was again happy he was there."

Self-Healing and Self-Acceptance. Many CMT participants have had spiritual experiences in which they were able to achieve a deeper level of self-acceptance, and perhaps to arrive at a healing space. Nancy wrote of her learning to trust her higher consciousness:

"What has started to happen for me is that I've begun to let go of the need to know; I've begun to trust enough that there is a 'higher power' or intelligence that is working on my behalf, that I can allow myself to be present in each moment. I've started to feel that perhaps my soul is recoverable, that I can access my own truth and live and act from it despite the risks of disapproval, or even rejection.

"With CMT I relaxed into a spaciousness I never knew was there. It seemed that every hope or expectation I had ever had was simply a void I was afraid to face. As I painted I moved closer to these voids, through the spaces and to the other side. Today I can lean back and not drown. I can let reality happen and feel the wonderful release from the limitation of fear. I can stop controlling and let life happen. I can do life and become who I am here, now, today, in this moment....

"Today I love myself unconditionally. My journey into painting thoughtlessly, mindlessly, and messily has been a journey back to myself. I have a greater sense of wholeness and purity."

David used his CMT experience as the basis of a paper he wrote for a course in consciousness studies at Holy

"Only a unifying experience that establishes anew a sense of wholeness as a principle working within the person can have a lastingly healing effect."

- Ira Progoff, Psychologist

Names College in Oakland, California:

"What I have learned from CMT ... is a more meaningful approach to life, a deeper and more coherent path, a regained sense of my place in nature, and ways that I can find my place when I lose my way. 'No-thought Mess Painting' has helped me to accept the process of my life, that I needn't be 'unhappy about being unhappy' or 'angry at being angry,' but rather to let my process be what it is. I can't be trying to push at myself to change. I can ask, but the answer will take its own course. Every time I cycle round to learn this lesson once again, this teaching sinks in more deeply."

Images of Transcendence. As with Janice Crow's Dark Shaman, Dunstan's crosses, or Bruce's mandalas (described in Chapter 7), many CMT participants find profoundly meaningful images emerging in their painting sessions. One client described a series of symbolic images that persistently reappeared in session after session:

"This experience plunged me into the depths of a deprivation I experienced in infancy — nursing at breasts which held very little milk. After painting hundreds of breasts, I finally painted black breasts which at the time I felt represented resignation to the fact that the milk was not there.

"However, as I continued to do Mess Paintings and more black breasts, I was overwhelmed with the realization that the black breasts were The Bosom of Death. A rush of suicidal feelings engulfed me — something I had never experienced before. As I continued to paint, the red paint cried out for life, while the black paint demanded death. The experience was full of despair and terror.

"Just as the black seemed about to engulf the red, the other colors insisted on being heard from, and in that moment of hopelessness, a painting of a beautiful spiral emerged. The spiral contained red and black — and every other color in the rainbow. And I finally felt at peace.

"The experience was so overwhelming that I felt a need to understand it better. And so, I researched it, to try to find out why the experience went from deprivation about the breast to suicidal despair to the spiral ... and I learned that the infant's experiences with the breast are connected with death wishes,

that suicidal despair can lead to transformation, and that the spiral symbolizes the reconciliation of life and death."

Universal Connectedness. Perhaps the most general statement that can be made about spirituality is that it involves a sense of wholeness and connectedness to everything that is. Many of the special CMT paintings that I have described in this book have been expressions of a transpersonal spiritual awareness that emerges and is affirmed in the paintings — for example, Marty's Orca images, or Dunstan's crosses.

Artist Wolfgang Paalen has eloquently summed up the power of painting to evoke the unification of the microcosm and the macrocosm:

"As music (it dissolves time) is given to man for his dialogue with eternity, painting is the adventure into an inner space which can not be measured by yardsticks nor light-years. A space where thought travels faster than light, where the nearest is also the farthest, where the smallest sea-shell curves are as meaningful as the galactic spiral and the eye of the mind at once beholds worlds gone and to come."

CMT has enabled many participants to open the door into this inner space and to embrace the spark of divinity that resides within all living beings.

Epilogue

Continuing Your Journey

Reviewing Your CMT Experience

At the end of your seven weeks of painting, I encourage you to go back and review all of your work, as well as the Checklists, Journal notes, and Dream Diary entries that accompanied each of your painting sessions. If you have kept good records, you will have a verbal and visual record of your inner states for 500 or so two-minute periods of painting.

In my CMT groups I ask my clients to write a formal final review paper. The review process may take them six or seven hours. If you choose to do this kind of review and then write a summary of your observations, you may find yourself experiencing even further breakthroughs.

As you look through your paintings and your written notes, you may find it useful to ask yourself some of the following questions:

- What were your hopes and expectations of CMT?
- How did your expectations compare with the results?
- What was the first week like?
- What was difficult for you?
- What surprised you?
- How did the paintings change?
- What did you learn about yourself?
- Did any of your relationships change?

- Did you change any attitudes or clarify any values?
- Did you change your behavior in any way?
- Did you begin any new activities?
- Did you reactivate old interests?
- Did you learn anything to apply to other areas of your life?
- Were there any physiological changes — for example, in sleep patterns, health problems, smoking, or drinking?
- Were there any psychological changes (for example, your level of hostility, fear, grief?)

For some of my clients, the final review has been a most enlightening experience. As they compiled notes to write a final summary, they arrived at additional insights, and sometimes spiritual awakenings. Recognizing and recording any changes that may have occurred during the weeks of Mess Painting, no matter how minor, can reinforce the benefits you have obtained with CMT and encourage additional beneficial changes to blossom in the future.

> *"We work at our own growth in order to move further along our path toward being at home with ourselves, with others, and with the universe. But the path is endless and there are always further vistas and possibilities ahead."*
>
> - Lawrence LeShan

Enjoying Your Mess Paintings

I have already mentioned some of the ways that people have made use of their Mess Paintings and displayed them after finishing their CMT program. Paul, the psychiatrist, used his paintings as gift wrappings. Many Mess Painters have matted and framed some of their favorite paintings. Honoring your work in this way, and observing it on your walls day after day, is a powerful expression of self-affirmation.

Not only whole paintings, but also parts of them, can become an endless source of delight. If you use small mats of various dimensions, it will be easy to create borders around interesting areas of your Mess Paintings and discover pieces that are well worth preserving.

Pieces of Mess Paintings can be used as book covers, or greeting cards. My editor Kathy Goss made what she called "Desert Shadow Boxes." She mounted fragments of Mess Paintings in ancient, rusty sardine cans, and then added fragments of bone, feathers, and dried plant parts that convey the feeling of the California high desert where she makes her home.

Going on with CMT

I urge you to consider continuing to paint, perhaps in an evening class in whatever medium attacts you. Many Mess Painters choose to take the CMT program again. Others leave their Mess Painting setup intact and continue to paint on their own when they feel the need. As Janice Crow observed in her four CMT programs, each repetition of the program has unique benefits and provides unique inner experiences. The spiral keeps turning, and with each go-around with CMT we continue to grow. Karen, another Mess Painter, observed: *"No matter how many times one does CMT, it is always useful, but in very different ways."*

Going through the anxious, fearful, angry, joyous, tranquil, boring, meditative, and ecstatic sessions of CMT does not make one creative forever after. Any widening of consciousness may eventually be followed by a feeling of being stifled. New challenges and new stresses will indicate a need for more CMT, or for involvement with other techniques for self-renewal.

The time of Mess Painting will come to a close, but the need for more of it, or for something similar on the next turn of your spiral of growth, is never over. Sometime in the future you will undoubtedly encounter a situation that brings up feelings of being patronized, unappreciated, or manipulated; or an illness or accident may threaten to dissolve your newly acquired strength. Some piece of old pain or rage, previously hidden in the memory bank, may come to the surface. It makes sense to learn additional appropriate ways to take care of anger and fear, so that you and others are not hurt. In the meantime, Mess Painting can always provide a safe place of containment, a place to let your feelings speak, to let them out, respect them, and allow them to have their say through color and form until the roaring quiets down.

> *"We shall not cease from exploration,*
> *And the end of all our exploring*
> *Will be to arrive where we started*
> *And know the place for the first time."*
> - T.S. Eliot, "Little Gidding," in *Four Quartets*

Getting Help: A Final Note

For CMT Participants. If you get started on your own with this book and would like my help with questions or concerns that arise, please write to me for information on the necessary financial arrangements. Please do not forward your questions before receiving instructions from me on how to proceed.

For Health Professionals, Art Therapists and Art Teachers. As a professional, after you have completed a CMT program you are entitled to study to become a certified facilitator. Write to the below address to request a brochure. Please include a self-addressed, stamped envelope.

Virginia Barclay Goldstein
c/o T.H.I.S.
P.O. Box 2344
Sausalito, California 94966 USA

Annotated Bibliography

Blumberger, Steven R., M.D. *An Overview of the Method, Theory and Outcome of the Creativity Technique,* a paper presented at the fourth annual conference of the National Association for Creative Children and Adults, Toronto, Canada, 1977.

Bradbury, Ray. *Zen and the Art of Writing.* Santa Barbara: Capra Press, 1973.

> This book is Bradbury's explanation of exactly what makes a writer a master of the craft. He does this so simply that the material may even appear to be *over* simplification. In addition, since all competent writers really write what they know, he makes it clear why a writer needs to know his or her own subconscious. In twenty-four pages he has put together an essay that is a thought-provoking little gem.

***The Brain/Mind Bulletin.* Marilyn Ferguson**, editor. P.O. Box 42211, Los Angeles, CA 90042.

> A packet of what this important Bulletin has published on creativity is available for a fee. Write to the above address.

British Autogenic Society. http://www.autogenic-therapy.org.uk

> The British Autogenic Society website is an excellent resource for anyone wishing to explore Autogenic Training. It includes information on the origins, theory, and applications of AT, standard and advanced

AT exercises, and referrals to practitioners. I will be presenting a master class in the UK on CMT, sponsored by The British Autogenic Society, in conjunction with the publication of *The Magic of Mess Painting*.

Csikszentmihalyi, Mihaly. *Flow: the Psychology of Optimal Experience*. New York: Harper & Row, 1990.

What makes us happy, glad to be alive? What experiences make life worthwhile? Czikszentimihalyi's scientific research on optimal experiences has gone on for over twenty years, and the implications for our individual lives are many. This is not a collection of do's and don'ts for happiness. Instead it is *"a voyage through the mind, charted with the tools of science."* Happiness is not something that is controlled by outside circumstances; it is something that comes from the inside — from our reactions to the experience. The author presents examples of how life can be made more enjoyable, and explains how this can be accomplished.

Dissanayake, Ellen. *Homo Aestheticus: Where Art Comes From and Why.* New York: Free Press, 1992.

This intellectually stimulating book advances a fascinating argument. Instead of aesthetic appreciation being something we learn or acquire, Dissanayake makes a strong case that artistic endeavors are a basic human drive. Art in its many forms has been universally practiced throughout all societies. Her thesis is well developed, interesting, and holds potential for enriching all our lives. It's refreshing to come across a new perspective.

Estes, Clarissa Pinkola. *Women Who Run with the Wolves: Myths and Stories of the Wild Woman Archetype*. New York: Ballantine, 1992.

Turn loose a master storyteller who is also a superb Jungian analyst, give her a first-class background from childhood with myth makers and myths, and you will find a power in her written word equal to that in her spoken word. Each of the nineteen myths in this book could stand on the merits of the story alone, but Estes also explains the meanings and the ramifications of each one very clearly. As she expands on the stories, as she deepens the reader's understanding, Estes passes on her wisdom so that it resonates within the reader. This book is challenging, inspiring, fascinating.

Goldstein, Virginia Barclay, and Greene, Michael J. *CMT: Creativity Mobilization Technique.* A sixteen-millimeter color documentary film with camerawork by Larry Hope and Gordon Mueller. San Francisco: 1978.

CMT: Creativity Mobilization Technique was reviewed favorably in *The Arts and Psychotherapy,* Vol. 7, p. 294, USA: Ancho International Inc., 1980; and by Stanley Krippner, PhD, of the Humanistic Psychology Institute, San Francisco. Krippner wrote :

"The film portrays CMT accurately. The color and sound are excellent, and psychologist Gay Luce's narration is superb. The value of CMT for stress reduction is extolled and case studies are presented. The video is highly recommended to art therapists and to others who acknowledge the value of creative expression not only in psychotherapy but as a tool to awaken human potentiality in general."

For information on how to order a video of *CMT: Creativity Mobilization Technique,* please write to Virginia Barclay Goldstein, c/o T.H.I.S., P.O. Box 2344, Sausalito, CA 94966.

Hillman, James and Ventura, Michael. *We've had a Hundred Years of Psychotherapy: And the World's Getting Worse.* San Francisco: Harper and Row, 1992.

Anyone who is interested in Jungian psychology probably knows of James Hillman. Here he enters into a series of dialogues with Michael Ventura, a columnist from the *L.A. Weekly,* including the letters they exchanged. It makes for a lively format. These are two very intelligent, very articulate people reflecting on what they have learned over their lifetimes. In doing so they not only take a fresh look at psychiatry but also at our society, our beliefs, our tunnel vision, our lives. It is stimulating, controversial, and well worth reading.

Hobson, J. Allan. *The Dreaming Brain*. New York: Basic Books, Inc., 1988.

The author is Professor of Psychiatry and Director of the Laboratory of Neurophysiology at Harvard Medical School. He reviews the history of the investigation of dreams in the nineteenth and twentieth centuries, as well as current research on dreaming. Neurobiology now has the capacity to study the functional activity of the brain cells, which has the potential to open up entire new theories of dream science. Hobson proposes an hypothesis that he calls an activation-synthesis model. He suggests that: *"REM sleep and dreaming include both the development and the active maintenance of the functional integrity of the human mind-brain. Much more than recovering from the wear and tear of today, tonight's sleep may be an active and dynamic preparation for the challenges of tomorrow."* Of additional interest are excerpts from an actual dream journal to illustrate his hypothesis. This is an academic book, but written in language intended to reach lay people as well as the scientific community.

London, Peter. *No More Secondhand Art: Awakening the Artist Within*. Boston: Shambhala, 1989.

Peter London is a practicing art therapist who is also Professor of Art Education at Southeastern Massachusetts University. In this book he uses his teaching skills to demonstrate that *"artistic process is more than a collection of crafted things; it is more than the process of creating those things."* London claims that if one will use creative expression it can not only change the look of one's art, it can change the quality of one's life. He goes on to provide twelve creative encounters, explaining how to do each encounter yourself. Throughout, London offers an expanded view of art and of alternative ways to see ourselves as artists. His final chapter on media is as refreshing and worth reading as the rest of the book.

Luthe, Wolfgang, M. D. *The Creativity Mobilization Technique*. New York: Grune & Stratton, 1976 (out of print).

Wolfgang Luthe, the creator of CMT, was a research physician with an international reputation. Originally the method was designed for use with his medical patients. When it became obvious that his painting process was equally useful for anyone wishing to unblock and develop creative potentials, Luthe wrote this textbook to be used at the college and graduate school levels. Both the method and the resulting phases of development are covered in great detail. Because of some publisher's errors and the compexity of Luthe's prose, this book has unfortunately not proven useful as a "how-to" text. It still serves, however as a valuable reference resource on creativity, with 265 entries on that subject in the Bibliography.

Meader, Jonathan. *In Praise of Women*. Berkeley: Celestial Arts, 1997.

To celebrate women throughout history, In Praise of Women combines stunning photographs of sculptures of women and insightful text, weaving a beautiful and unique vision. The striking images are complemented by poetry and prose, carefully chosen to add even greater dimension to the sculptures, and they evoke wonderful moods and emotions: eroticism, maternity, grace, strength, humor, pathos, gentleness, passion and love. The viewer is transported to another time, another place, to be in the presence of incredible women.

Miller, Alice. *Pictures of a Childhood*. New York: Farrar, Straus & Giroux, 1986.

Dr. Miller, an outstanding psychoanalyst, has made ground-breaking studies of child abuse and of the misguided notions of what constitutes a "good upbringing." After many years of devotion to her profession, Miller finally found the time to paint. She had the theory that creative work, such as that done by painters and poets, is often the expression of forgotten early childhood trauma. As she began to *"play with colors in a totally spontaneous way"* she found what two analyses had not given her — her own long-forgotten memories of her childhood, and an accompanying freedom that she had never experienced before. The book contains sixty-six of her watercolors and a remarkable essay.

Miller, Henry. *The Paintings of Henry Miller: Paint as You Like and Die Happy.* Edited by Noel Young. San Francisco: Chronicle Books, 1982.

The subtitle is the title of one of the four essays by Miller which are included along with seventy-eight watercolors, spanning some five decades, selected out of the thousands he did during his lifetime. The other three essays are: "To Paint is To Love Again," "The Waters Reglitterized," and "The Painting Lesson." Miller spent almost as much time painting as he did writing, and those interested in CMT will particularly enjoy the watercolors. Each painting was to Miller an adventure, and his joy in them is contagious. If you need inspiration, here it is.

Morrissey, Dunstan. *To Hear Thoroughly: Father Dunstan Morrissey Talks About His Life.* Edited by Susan Moon. 1998: Open Books, 1631 Grant Street, Berkeley CA 94703, (510) 548-2208.

This delightful little book describes the remarkable life of a Benedictine monk who embraced a life of solitude and founded a spiritual retreat center in Sonoma County, California. As a CMT participant, Dunstan Morrissey recognized that this painting process provided spiritual benefits similar to the monastic practice of solitude.

Nachmanovitch, Stephen. *Free Play: Improvisation in Life and Art.* New York: Tarcher/Putnam, 1990.

Drawing upon his experience as an improvising musician, Nachmanovitch eloquently explores the origins of and impediments to the creative process. A must read for all Mess Painters, this inspiring text emphasizes the importance of flow, or letting go; recognizes the spiritual sources of creativity; and celebrates creativity as a life-enhancing process for laymen and professional artists alike. Profuse quotations and illustrations from master artists, as well an excellent bibliography, entice the reader into further exploration.

Pear, Marcia. *What You Need to Know -- A Road Map for Personal Transformation.* Marcia Pear, 1998. http://www.peaksuccess.com

An inspirational 62 minute spoken-word adventure (with background music) that guides you on a personal pilgrimage home to your heart. Available on CD or cassette. Contact: The Center for Creative Change, P.O. Box 2258, Sebastopol, CA 95473. (707) 522-9529.

Steinem, Gloria. *Revolution from Within: A Book of Self-Esteem.* Boston: Little, Brown and Co., 1991.

Steinem presents a clear and inspiring description of self-esteem and of possible ways of achieving more of it. Having been in the forefront of women's struggle for equality, Gloria Steinem came to an increasingly clear realization that outside power, even with equality, is not enough — neither for women nor for men. Societal change imposed from the outside works only short-term, if at all, unless accompanied by inner change. Using research, reports, and parables from personal lives (her own included), Steinem manages to convey very clearly the value of this "inner revolution." Anyone involved with CMT will recognize with delight how appropriately the painting method applies to exactly what is being said in these chapters.

Theroux, Alexander. *The Primary Colors.* New York: Henry Holt, 1994.

In this collection of three dazzling essays, Theroux explores the complex connotations of the three primary colors — blue, yellow, and red — in a free-form, encyclopedic meditation on their associations in art, history, music, poetry, fiction, movies, anthropology, linguistics, myth, religion, science, food, sports, and everyday life. Currently out of print, but worth looking for.

Index